Leadership *for*
Growing Churches

Leadership *for* Growing Churches

Paul's Recipe for
Prospering the Church in Crete

Clarence Bouwman

WIPF *&* STOCK · Eugene, Oregon

LEADERSHIP FOR GROWING CHURCHES
Paul's Recipe for Prospering the Church in Crete

Wipf & Stock
An Imprint of Wipf and Stock Publishers
199 W. 8th Ave., Suite 3
Eugene, OR 97401

www.wipfandstock.com

PAPERBACK ISBN: 978-1-4982-3388-0
HARDCOVER ISBN: 978-1-4982-3390-3

Manufactured in the U.S.A.

*Dedicated to
the brothers and sisters in the Orient
where so much needs to be done
to impart the whole counsel of God*

*—and to the brothers and sisters of the West
where so much needs to be done
to embrace again the whole counsel of God*

Contents

Preface

BOOKS ON SUCCESSFUL BUSINESS leadership abound. But how do you lead a church? Can one simply impose a business model on church leaders and expect the church to flourish?

It would seem not. Though the Apostle Paul penned his letter to Titus long before modern leadership gurus wrote their tomes, Paul's work has the singular distinction of being inspired by none less than the Holy Spirit of the very Christ who gathers, defends, and preserves his church. That can only mean that anyone who would seek to provide fitting leadership in the church must of necessity take Paul's instruction about church leadership seriously.

This publication seeks to assist today's reader as he works his way through Paul's letter to Titus. Along the way we'll grapple with questions as:

- What ought leadership in a church to look like?
- What role are individual members to play in the Lord's church?
- How do you make a church prosper?
- How does one handle dissent in a church?
- How does the church thrive in a culture of deceit?

A fresh look at this letter's answers can only be beneficial as the church seeks to function God's way in today's business-minded world.

Acknowledgements

It is fitting that I express a word of appreciation to particular persons and parties, without whose assistance this work would never have seen the light of day. My ever-dedicated wife, Arlene, has unfailingly stood beside me as helper in the task the Lord has given me. That reality has given me the space and the encouragement to complete this publication. I thank the Lord for her. Our children too, be they still at home or already out of the parental nest, have been and continue to be a source of joy and encouragement. I gratefully acknowledge their contribution to my work.

The consistory and congregation of the Canadian Reformed Church of Smithville have also contributed abundantly to this project. I thank them for their stimulating responses to the sermons I delivered on the letter to Titus. Congregation and consistory alike also came to understand that Titus has much to say in today's world, and so readily granted me time away from my regular work to complete this project. I am in your debt.

A number of very capable experts found time in their busy schedules to read carefully through an earlier version of this publication. I publicly thank Arjan de Visser, George W. Knight, Nelson D. Kloosterman, William den Hollander Sr, and Gerhard H. Visscher for their engaging interactions. Needless to say, the final version is my responsibility.

Every work needs its editors. Jolene Bouwman and Amanda Ellens toiled their way through my writing in an effort to remove grammatical weaknesses and spelling errors. Ryan Kampen

Acknowledgements

assisted graciously with further editorial work and compiled the indices. Thank you so very much for your diligent labors!

With the work now completed, I thank the Lord my God for the privilege to serve in his kingdom in the capacity he has granted. It is my prayer that the Lord will bless this work, to the benefit of his churches and the greater glory of his most wonderful Name.

Introduction

BY THE GRACE OF God, the gospel of Jesus Christ had come to the residents of the island of Crete, and as a result a number of Cretans came to faith. Their coming to faith, obviously, did not mean that all church building work was now done in their midst—as if church building only involves bringing in new converts. The Apostle Paul understood that much needed to be done to enhance church life on the island. So Paul did two things. First, he "left" Titus on the island to "put what remained into order" (Titus 1:5).[1] Thereafter he wrote Titus a letter with details as to how Titus should fulfill this mandate.

Titus has long since finished his earthly sojourn and received from God the crown of glory. The same Lord, however, has seen fit to preserve Paul's letter to Titus—and even had it be included in Holy Scripture—so that we today might use this same instruction to ensure that the churches to which we belong be organized in a fashion that pleases the Lord. With that purpose in mind, I propose to take the reader through Paul's letter to Titus in order to set forth the Lord's intent for what his church ought to look like through the centuries.

Simply reading Paul's letter to Titus, however, is not by itself going to show us how the Lord would have his churches function. Preachers also need to communicate Paul's instructions to Titus to their congregations. How, concretely, does one do that? Before

---

1. All quotations are taken from the English Standard Version, unless otherwise indicated.

we begin to read Titus together, I want to devote some attention to how preachers today ought to prepare sermons on this letter. That is Part 1 of this publication. In Part 2 we will read Paul's letter to Titus with the benefit of the principles learned in Part 1. For the benefit of those who wish to use this publication for study purposes, discussion questions follow each chapter.

Every project has a context, and this publication does too. Some four years ago the Lord directed my path as preacher of the gospel to a church of nearly six hundred members. Together with fourteen elders and seven deacons I was to function as pastor and teacher in this large flock. It was quickly obvious to me that the ship of this church could float only when all hands were on deck, contributing to the needs of the saints. As I considered how to address this need in the congregation, my attention was drawn to Paul's letter to Titus. The further I got into the letter, the more I was persuaded that here was material that had much to say to today's (larger) churches. Being rightly organized is vital to functioning well! Surely one cannot expect God's blessing to rest on the work one does in the church if one ignores God's own instruction on how he wants his churches run. Needless to say, the effort to get the church organized as ought, and then to keep the church organized as ought, is ongoing work; it shall not finally be complete until the day of the Lord's return.

Part 1

Preaching from Titus

Chapter 1

Making the Sermon

TITUS RECEIVED A LETTER from Paul with specific instructions about what steps he was to take to ensure that the work begun in Crete be completed as the Lord wished it to be. We can imagine that as Titus sought to carry out his mandate, he travelled from town to town to appoint elders (Titus 1:5). More, as he travelled he surely will have made it his business to "teach what is in accord with sound doctrine" (2:1), and have done so with words of encouragement and rebuke (2:15), and all the while flavored his messages with reminders (3:1) and insistence (3:8). But what, we wonder, would Titus' teaching—his sermons—have sounded like? What resources would he have used to prepare those sermons? We would love to look over his shoulder as he labored in his study, and love also to listen in as he delivered the fruits of his studies. How much we would benefit, we feel, from such an experience!

The Lord has not preserved for our instruction any of the sermons Titus preached. That does not, however, leave us in the dark in answering the question at hand. With but little imagination we can visit Titus in his study as he pores over his books and manuscripts to prepare his sermons. What do we see?

Titus at Work

Spread before Titus is first of all the letter he received from Paul. Elsewhere on his desk is a copy of the Old Testament—likely in Greek (see Gal 2:3). Though Titus lives and preaches in the New Testament dispensation, we notice his Old Testament is well used and worn.

Why do I picture a well-worn Old Testament on Titus' desk? I do so because Titus is Paul's "true child in a common faith" (Titus 1:4). That undoubtedly means at a minimum that Titus knows how Paul's mind works. He knows that as the Apostle busies himself with what needs to be done to grow the fledgling church in Crete, he will be studying God's earlier revelation diligently to find God's will. To follow Paul's thoughts as recorded in the letter he received, Titus obviously needs to study the same material Paul studied.

Paul

What makes me so confident that Paul studied the Old Testament as he prepared his letter to Titus? Consider the following:

- From his childhood Paul (then Saul of Tarsus) had been steeped in the Scriptures God had revealed thus far, namely, the Old Testament. In the course of his studies under Professor Gamaliel (Acts 22:3), he increased in Old Testament knowledge beyond his fellow students (Gal 1:14).

- We may safely assume that as he grew up and continued his studies, Saul read widely not only from the Old Testament and existing works and commentaries on it, but also from the Greek literature available in his day; he could, after all, freely quote from the Greek poet Epimenides in Titus 1:12.

- Saul was a student in Jerusalem during the time of Jesus' earthly ministry. We do not know whether he ever met Jesus personally, but it is beyond a doubt that this bright student was as aware of Jesus' words and works as any other Pharisee in the city. Saul, however, did not accept that Jesus was the promised Messiah and therefore the fulfillment of the Scriptures. So convinced was he that Jesus was a false teacher that he consented to Stephen's stoning (Acts 8:1) and led the effort to eradicate those who followed the Way (Acts 9:1, 2; see also Acts 26:9–11).

- After his conversion on the road to Damascus, Paul straightaway understood that Jesus was "Lord" (Acts 9:5) and so was the fulfillment of Old Testament prophecy. As a result "immediately he proclaimed Jesus in the synagogues, saying, 'he is the Son of God'" (Acts 9:20) and "proving that Jesus was the Christ" (Acts 9:22). Here his extensive training in the Old Testament and his prior intimate knowledge of Jesus' teaching and work bore instant fruit; at his conversion the penny dropped so that God's revelation in the Old Testament and its fulfillment in Jesus Christ now made complete sense to him. Of course, as the years went by, his insight into how Jesus fulfilled Old Testament Scripture will have deepened.

Following Paul's Thought

Titus was an early associate of the Apostle Paul (Gal 2:1), and over the years witnessed Paul at work, heard his preaching, and followed his discussions. In the process Titus learned from this man—steeped as he was in the Old Testament—how to work with those ancient Scriptures in the post-Calvary and post-Pentecost era. As Titus, then, set himself to preparing sermons on the material Paul mentioned in the letter he received, he could follow *why* his spiritual father told him to teach what he had to teach. He understood that there was a *flow-on* from any given Old Testament passage through to the audience in Crete. This flow-on had the following stations:

- God's revelation in a given Old Testament passage came first to a particular audience, in a particular historical context, and was subsequently written into sacred Scripture. For example, the Passover instruction in Exodus 12:1–28 was revealed to the Israelites on a particular night a dozen centuries earlier, and for a specific reason.

- Later Old Testament Scripture expanded on, clarified, and/ or fulfilled what God had revealed in an earlier passage. For example, some months after Israel's arrival at Mt. Sinai, God instructed Moses to elaborate on his revelation about the Passover (Lev 23:4–8; Num 28:16–25). There could potentially be multiple expansions or clarifications as the years went by. So Moses said more about the Passover after the forty-year sojourn in the desert ended (Deut 16:1–8), and Josiah (2 Chron 35), Ezra (6:19–22), and Ezekiel (45:21–24) recorded still more about this sacrament many years later. These expansions as well were addressed to particular audiences and occurred in specific historical contexts.

- Jesus Christ fulfilled all God's earlier revelation (Jesus' words in Matthew 5:17 were no secret to Paul or to Titus). His instruction during his three-year public ministry expanded on his Father's Old Testament revelation, and clarified what was not sufficiently clear to his hearers within their particular setting. On the matter of the Passover, for example, Jesus celebrated it with his disciples and instituted a replacement sacrament (Matt 26:17–30).

- After Jesus' triumph on Calvary and exaltation into heaven, he gave his servants deep and clear insight into God's Old Testament revelation through his poured-out Spirit. This insight drew out how the Scriptures were fulfilled in him (John 16:13, 14). Peter's sermon on the day of Pentecost serves as a clear example (Acts 2:14–36). The Holy Spirit led the post-Pentecost church to act and speak in a certain way in relation to Lord's Supper (Acts 2:42).

- Paul was mandated to carry Jesus' name to Gentiles and Jews alike (Acts 9:15). In fulfilling that mandate, he digested God's Old Testament revelation through the fulfillment in Jesus Christ, and, under the guidance of the Holy Spirit, applied it within the context of his hearers in their actual daily setting.

To stay with the example of the Passover, Paul applied its ongoing significance to the Corinthians in their specific circumstances in 1 Corinthians 5:6–8 and elsewhere.

• Titus received Paul's (inspired) instruction, and went to work with it in the concrete circumstances of Crete. As it turns out, there is no direct reference to the Passover in his letter. If there had been, though, Titus would have had to take seriously (as any preacher expositing 1 Corinthians 5:6–8 discernibly must) all the above-mentioned Old Testament passages on the Passover as well as what Jesus did and said about the sacrament and how the post-Pentecost church had carried out this instruction thus far.

For Titus to be effective, then, as he unpacked Paul's instruction for the benefit of the Christians of Crete, he needed to:

• Know the circumstances of his hearers. He must, in other words, stand in their shoes so that he knew their needs and heard as they would hear.

• Know Paul's manner of thinking so that he could follow why Paul wrote what he wrote.

• Know how Jesus had fulfilled particular (Old Testament) Scripture passages and what that fulfillment meant for the post-Pentecost church.

• Know how later Old Testament Scripture expanded upon and clarified earlier Scripture.

• Understand the relevant Old Testament passages Paul was building on, and how those passages were themselves (possibly) built upon a deeper foundation in revelation given earlier still.

Spanning all of this is the conviction that God Almighty stands unchangingly above changing times and ages. He is the one constant, who has slowly but surely revealed his will through a series of multiple stages and in differing circumstances through the generations. As Titus grappled with how to bring God's word to bear on the lives of the Cretan believers, he had to wander far beyond the single text in Paul's letter that he wanted to expound. To do justice to Paul's words, Titus had to dig beneath the text of what Paul wrote to penetrate the material that formed Paul's thinking. In short, Titus had to work with the entirety of Scripture.

Of course, any preacher living after Titus adds one more step in this process: he has to get into Titus' skin and follow his thoughts as he unpacks the letter to Titus for the benefit of a twenty-first-century audience. In so doing he needs to recognize that the Holy Spirit has given a complete second Testament—so that the preacher expounding Paul's letter to Titus must not only look *back* (into the Old Testament, the days of Jesus and the early church), but also look *around* (into Paul's other letters as well as those of the other apostles) and even look *forward* (into the prophecy of Revelation and even what the Lord has done in the course of church history).

Preaching Titus

What does this mean for how we preach on Titus?

- A given text from Paul's letter to Titus is never a *dot-devoid-of-context* upon which a preacher may comment with remarks applicable to today's needs. From a dot you can draw lines in any direction. But if you draw lines from a dot into any direction you wish, your application can come across as unfounded and subjective, and therefore lacking scriptural authority. In fact, then you can say equally "true" things based on a well-formulated sentence of a newspaper article, or an agreeable paragraph from Confucius or from Hitler's *Mein Kampf*.

- Scripture is the word of the unchanging God who spans the ages. This means that one passage of Scripture—say a text from Titus—must be read in light of God's earlier revelation. So a given text in Titus is always a *dot-on-a-line*, with the line formed by multiple dots of revelation over the ages, each dot having its own specific context. Recall what I wrote above about the Passover. As the preacher traces the line through the dots he needs to understand the context of each dot.

Note: the preacher needs to pick out only those details of each dot that are relevant to the line he is following through the multiple dots. The point here is that multiple lines can travel through any given dot—and the preacher needs to be wary of getting sidetracked by other lines traveling through the same text.

- Once the preacher has connected multiple dots through the span of God's revelation (including texts from various periods of the Old Testament, Jesus' time, and the history of revelation up to and including the apostles' day), he will see where the trajectory of the line he has drawn points in terms of today's hearers. Application built on the trajectory of these connected dots is no longer subjective (and therefore potentially lame), but has objective credibility and even divine authority. To be clear: this does not make the message of today's preachers "inspired" or "infallible" as the writings of Holy Scripture are, but recognizes the blessed consequence of using Scripture correctly.

In the expositional part of this book, I will attempt to do two things. Obviously, I will try to explain what Paul wrote to Titus. But I will also try to stand beside Titus in an effort to follow his thoughts as he digests what his spiritual father (Titus 1:4) wrote to him. Invariably, then, the pages that follow will contain much Old Testament material as well as material drawn from Jesus' instruction and even from the early church.

I should perhaps then also be upfront: the bulk of the material that follows is the result of preaching through the letter to Titus in my current congregation. Typically the sermons fell into three predictable parts:

- The first part looked back into God's earlier revelation on the topic Paul was writing about; here I studied alongside Titus the Old Testament material that formed Paul's thinking on the topic.

- The second part looked closely at what Paul himself wrote to Titus on the particular topic Paul raised; here I attempted to hear what Titus-on-Crete would have heard in Paul's instruction and what it meant for the Cretan Christians.

- The third part followed the trajectory of the connected dots into today's circumstances in my current congregation.

Paul's Letter to Titus

I imagine that Titus on the island of Crete was doing his daily work in the churches when he received a letter from his spiritual father, Paul. I imagine too that he dropped all to read the letter, and read it again:[1]

> 1 Paul, a servant of God and an apostle of Jesus Christ, for the sake of the faith of God's elect and their knowledge of the truth, which accords with godliness, 2 in hope of eternal life, which God, who never lies, promised before the ages began 3 and at the proper time manifested in his word through the preaching with which I have been entrusted by the command of God our Savior; 4 To Titus, my true child in a common faith: Grace and peace from God the Father and Christ Jesus our Savior.
>
> 5 This is why I left you in Crete, so that you might put what remained into order, and appoint elders in every town as I directed you— 6 if anyone is above reproach, the husband of one wife, and his children are believers and not open to the charge of debauchery or insubordination. 7 For an overseer, as God's steward, must be above reproach. He must not be arrogant or quick-tempered or a drunkard or violent or greedy for gain, 8 but hospitable, a lover of good, self-controlled, upright, holy, and disciplined. 9 He must hold firm to the trustworthy word as taught, so that he may be able

---

1. Paul's letters had no chapter or verse divisions. These were added many years later for reference purposes. As one reads Paul's letter to Titus, then, one does well to ignore the numbers buried in the text of the letter.

to give instruction in sound doctrine and also to rebuke those who contradict it.

10 For there are many who are insubordinate, empty talkers and deceivers, especially those of the circumcision party. 11 They must be silenced, since they are upsetting whole families by teaching for shameful gain what they ought not to teach. 12 One of the Cretans, a prophet of their own, said, "Cretans are always liars, evil beasts, lazy gluttons." 13 This testimony is true. Therefore rebuke them sharply, that they may be sound in the faith, 14 not devoting themselves to Jewish myths and the commands of people who turn away from the truth. 15 To the pure, all things are pure, but to the defiled and unbelieving, nothing is pure; but both their minds and their consciences are defiled. 16 They profess to know God, but they deny him by their works. They are detestable, disobedient, unfit for any good work.

2 But as for you, teach what accords with sound doctrine. 2 Older men are to be sober-minded, dignified, self-controlled, sound in faith, in love, and in steadfastness. 3 Older women likewise are to be reverent in behavior, not slanderers or slaves to much wine. They are to teach what is good, 4 and so train the young women to love their husbands and children, 5 to be self-controlled, pure, working at home, kind, and submissive to their own husbands, that the word of God may not be reviled. 6 Likewise, urge the younger men to be self-controlled. 7 Show yourself in all respects to be a model of good works, and in your teaching show integrity, dignity, 8 and sound speech that cannot be condemned, so that an opponent may be put to shame, having nothing evil to say about us. 9 Bondservants are to be submissive to their own masters in everything; they are to be well-pleasing, not argumentative, 10 not pilfering, but showing all good faith, so that in everything they may adorn the doctrine of God our Savior.

11 For the grace of God has appeared, bringing salvation for all people, 12 training us to renounce ungodliness and worldly passions, and to live self-controlled, upright, and godly lives in the present age, 13 waiting

for our blessed hope, the appearing of the glory of our great God and Savior Jesus Christ, **14** who gave himself for us to redeem us from all lawlessness and to purify for himself a people for his own possession who are zealous for good works.

15 Declare these things; exhort and rebuke with all authority. Let no one disregard you.

3 Remind them to be submissive to rulers and authorities, to be obedient, to be ready for every good work, **2** to speak evil of no one, to avoid quarreling, to be gentle, and to show perfect courtesy toward all people. **3** For we ourselves were once foolish, disobedient, led astray, slaves to various passions and pleasures, passing our days in malice and envy, hated by others and hating one another. **4** But when the goodness and loving kindness of God our Savior appeared, **5** he saved us, not because of works done by us in righteousness, but according to his own mercy, by the washing of regeneration and renewal of the Holy Spirit, **6** whom he poured out on us richly through Jesus Christ our Savior, **7** so that being justified by his grace we might become heirs according to the hope of eternal life. **8** The saying is trustworthy, and I want you to insist on these things, so that those who have believed in God may be careful to devote themselves to good works. These things are excellent and profitable for people. **9** But avoid foolish controversies, genealogies, dissensions, and quarrels about the law, for they are unprofitable and worthless. **10** As for a person who stirs up division, after warning him once and then twice, have nothing more to do with him, **11** knowing that such a person is warped and sinful; he is self-condemned.

12 When I send Artemas or Tychicus to you, do your best to come to me at Nicopolis, for I have decided to spend the winter there. **13** Do your best to speed Zenas the lawyer and Apollos on their way; see that they lack nothing. **14** And let our people learn to devote themselves to good works, so as to help cases of urgent need, and not be unfruitful.

15 All who are with me send greetings to you. Greet those who love us in the faith.

Grace be with you all.

Overview

That is the letter, short and to the point, yet with much for Titus to think about as he returned to his work. Perhaps he will have noticed that the letter could be broken down into several bite-size bits with each in turn providing access to specific instruction Paul's sender had given in earlier revelation. However that may have been, the following overview of the letter worked well for me as I laid the letter before the congregation:

1. Introduction (1:1–4)

2. Instruction #1—appoint elders (1:5–16)

3. Instruction #2—teach sound doctrine (2:1—3:11)

    a. In relation to groupings within the churches (2:1–15)

        i.   The older men (2:2)

        ii. The older women (2:3, 4a)

        iii. The younger women (2:4b, 5)

        iv. The younger men (2:6–8)

        v.   The slaves (2:9, 10)

        vi. The grounds for these instructions (2:11–14)

    b. In relation to observers from outside the churches (3:1–11)

        vii. Doing good in the neighborhood (3:1–8)

        viii. Avoiding foolish controversies (3:9–11)

4. Concluding matters (3:12–15)

    a. Pulling the preacher (3:12–14)

    b. Greetings (3:15)

POINTS FOR DISCUSSION

1. We acknowledge that the Holy Spirit inspired Paul to write this letter to Titus. How did that happen? Do you picture Paul in dead-brained fashion picking up his quill and then moving his hand to write word after word as the Holy Spirit moved him? Why or why not?

2. If you answer Question 1 with a No (as you ought to), what alternative process do you imagine Paul followed as he got himself ready to write his letter to Titus? Be prepared to justify your answer. Hint: check out Luke 1:1–4.

3. God's revelation in the early part of Scripture (say, Genesis) has been compared to a bulb, while his revelation in the later parts of Scripture (say, the epistles of the apostles) has been compared to the blooming flower. The sections in between, then, have been compared to progressive stages of the flower's development, from bud to bloom.

    a. Do you think this comparison is helpful? Explain your answer.

    b. How could this comparison help you to understand why Paul is continually busy with the Old Testament?

    c. What does this comparison say about how we today can work with the Old Testament?

4. Why does the text of a sermon need to come from the Bible, and not from a wise saying found in the writings of Confucius or Louis L'Amour? Explain your answer.

5. Consider the sermons you hear in your church Sunday by Sunday. Does the study behind the sermon treat the text as a "dot" in isolation from other Scripture, or does the sermon connect numerous scriptural "dots" to form a single "line"? Does it make a difference in how you receive the sermon? If so, how?

6. In your own Bible studies, do you treat the passage under discussion in isolation from earlier and later Scripture or in

conjunction with what came before and what follows? How would you evaluate your favorite commentaries in relation to this question?

7. We are daily confronted with the need to make choices, and so turn to the Bible to find answers. In some cases we find a direct instruction that translates obviously into today's situation. For example, the command not to kill human life speaks directly to the question of abortion. In other cases we struggle to find God's will for us. We find ourselves hard-pressed, for example, to find a text that addresses directly the question of whether a mother ought to hold down a full-time job while she has dependent children still at home. How do you use the Scripture, then, to find an answer to a question like that?

8. In your initial reading of Paul's letter to Titus, what allusions have you found to God's earlier revelation? Find some examples of where Paul is working with what he learned

    a. from Jesus (the gospels),

    b. from the prophets (the latter part of the Old Testament),

    c. from Moses (the first five books of the Old Testament).

Part 2

Unpacking Paul's Letter to Titus for Today's World

Chapter 2

The Introduction to the Letter

WE HAVE WITHIN THE body of Holy Scripture more than a dozen letters from the Apostle Paul. They all begin with an introduction of some form, mentioning such details as the author and the recipient(s). What is striking about Paul's short letter to Titus is its comparatively very lengthy and intricate introduction, 1:1–4.[1] Listen:

> Paul, a servant of God and an apostle of Jesus Christ, for the sake of the faith of God's elect and their knowledge of the truth, which accords with godliness, 2 in hope of eternal life, which God, who never lies, promised before the ages began 3 and at the proper time manifested in his word through the preaching with which I have been entrusted by the command of God our Savior;
> 4 To Titus, my true child in a common faith:
> Grace and peace from God the Father and Christ Jesus our Savior.
> 5 This is why I left you in Crete, so that you might put what remained into order . . .

One wonders why this introduction is so detailed and extensive. With his introduction the Apostle is laying the foundation

---

1. The only letter with an introduction as elaborate as Paul writes to Titus is in his letter to the Romans—and that letter is five times the length of this letter.

for what he intends to write in the body of his letter. Though we may be impatient to get to the heart of this letter—what needs yet to be completed to have a church run properly—Paul considers it important that Titus first have some fundamental principles straight in his mind. Titus was, of course, familiar with this material already; he was, after all, Paul's "true child in a common faith" (Titus 1:4). But if the churches in Crete were to benefit from Titus' labor, they had to know and accept the God-given authority with which their preacher did his work. Paul's foundational statement, then, provided Titus with essential preaching material.

Paul's Self-Description

The man writing this letter introduces himself as "Paul." From other passages of Scripture we know he was a Jew deeply schooled in the Old Testament. Though his letter to Titus (unlike most of Paul's other letters) contains no direct quotes from the Old Testament, Paul's thinking was molded by the upbringing he received as a child, his education in the synagogue, and his studies as the feet of Gamaliel—all of which were concentrated on the Old Testament (see Acts 22:3; Gal 1:14).

The Apostle was undoubtedly aware of Jesus' work and teaching during his student days in Jerusalem. Jesus, after all, did not do his work in secret, but—as he said at the moment of his arrest— "day after day I sat in the temple teaching" (Matt 26:55). Of course, in his pre-conversion days Paul did not accept that Jesus was the Messiah spoken of in the Old Testament; that realization did not come till Jesus confronted him on the road to Damascus. As far as Paul was concerned, he had all his life been a faithful "servant of God," the "God" of his upbringing, the God who revealed himself in the Old Testament. This is the God whom Paul knew to be real, the God for whom Paul was so zealous that he went out of his way to persecute those Jews who did not serve this God as Paul thought the Old Testament required (see Acts 8:3; Phil 3:6).

Servant of God

Paul calls himself "a servant of God"—as our translation has it. We do well to note that the Greek word used here actually describes a slave. A slave in Paul's day had no rights or liberties of his own, but was fully the property of his master—and therefore obligated to fulfill the master's wishes in return for the master's care and protection. The same phrase "servant of God" is applied in the Old Testament to Moses (Ps 105:26), David (2 Sam 7:5, 8; Ps 78:70), the prophets (Isa 20:3; Jer 7:25; 25:4; Amos 3:7), and other leaders (Hag 2:23). By applying this title to himself, Paul consciously placed himself in the same league as these Old Testament figures. As these leaders were expected to lead and teach the people of God in full agreement with God's ordinances revealed at Mt. Sinai (and clarified through the prophets in the generations that followed), so Paul was to unpack further what God had revealed in days gone by. He had no rights of his own that might allow him liberty to alter what God had said; as "slave of God" Paul was duty-bound to follow God's instructions to the letter. That Paul understood this very well is perhaps illustrated best by referencing his zeal for persecuting those who, by Paul's estimation, served this God wrongly (see Phil 3:6; Acts 26:9–11).

God's revelation in the Old Testament focused specifically on the relation between God and his people-by-covenant. Though the human race had once broken that relation through the fall into sin and so were exiled from God's presence (Gen 3:6, 23), God was pleased to establish his covenant of grace with the people of Israel (Exod 20:2) and live among them in the tabernacle (Exod 40:34). Holy God as he was, he condescended to live with sinful people in the tabernacle because one day the perfect Lamb of God, Jesus Christ, would offer himself to pay for sin on the cross of Calvary. The sacrifices repeatedly offered on the altar in front of the tabernacle foreshadowed this perfect sacrifice. It was the task of the priests and Levites to explain these daily sacrifices in light of this upcoming great Sacrifice (Lev 10:11). In Paul's own time, the Lamb of God had come in the flesh (John 1:29), atoned for sin, and reconciled sinners to God. After Jesus' ascension into heaven the triumphant Lamb of God arrested Paul on the road to Damascus and enlisted him to become his preacher to the Gentiles (Acts 9:5, 6). Now it was Paul's task to show his hearers how the sacrifices of the Old Testament had pointed forward to, and were fulfilled in, Jesus Christ the Savior of the world.

Apostle of Jesus Christ

It is no wonder, then, that Paul next referred to himself as "an apostle of Jesus Christ." As Lord of all and ruling from the right hand of the Father (Acts 2:33, 36), this Christ was able to seize any person he chose to be his tool. Paul had once been "breathing threats and murder against the disciples of the Lord" (9:1), yet this sovereign Christ had compelled even him to acknowledge the reality of Jesus' divine identity and victory. Paul, once a tormentor of the church, was now mandated to carry Christ's word "before Gentiles and kings and the children of Israel" (9:15).

The term "apostle" (from the Greek word for "to send") captures the thought that Paul was "sent" on this mission, with no option on his part to decline his appointment. As "slave of God" and "apostle of Jesus Christ," Paul was not his own man, saying or writing what he felt like saying. Rather, he said and wrote what the ascended Christ through his Spirit caused him to say. Behind Paul and his words was none less than the very Christ who laid down his life to save sinners, and whom God anointed as Lord over all. As *his* ambassador, one dare not ignore what Paul has to say—or argue with it.

Intent

Paul mentions the reason for his slavery to God and his apostleship to Jesus Christ. He was enslaved and sent "for the sake of the faith of God's elect and their knowledge of the truth, which accords with godliness." The phrase "for the sake of" catches the *purpose* of his mission.

Those who benefit are "God's elect," a term the Apostle borrows from the Old Testament. In passages such as 1 Chronicles 16:13, Psalm 105:6, 43, and Isaiah 65:9, the phrase is used to describe the people of God—those who tasted God's goodness and care. But the objects of God's care were not limited to Old Testament generations. His church-gathering work continues through all ages. In the New Testament dispensation, the Lord also has a people chosen to life. Paul acknowledges that he was one of God's instruments through whom he was pleased to build up the faith of his elect in that first generation after Jesus' victory and ascension. Paul's authority to contribute to the Lord's church-building work is plain: he had been sent "for the sake of the faith of God's elect" also in Crete, where so much work still needed to be done to organize the church rightly. Titus—and his hearers, too—would ignore Paul's instruction at their own peril.

Through Paul's work "the faith of God's elect" and "their knowledge of the truth" would be strengthened. These two objects of Paul's labor, "faith" and "knowledge," again both have roots in Old Testament Scripture. The term "faith" describes here one's trust (the act of believing), while the term "knowledge" refers to what one believes. The Psalms make clear that believers in fact struggle to trust God in the midst of life's storms, and at the same time demonstrate that the Lord always gives his own the strength needed to cling to his promises. The saints of Crete experienced the same sorts of struggles as the saints of centuries before, and so they needed to be encouraged and taught to trust God in all life's changing circumstances.

Again, the "knowledge" of the truth which accords with godliness is not some novel revelation unconnected to God's Word in the Old Testament, but is built on the work of Moses and those who followed him. The point is that, as Paul seeks to complete through Titus the Lord's church building work among the elect of God in Crete, he first exposes the foundation upon which he intends to build: God's revelation in the Old Testament. Titus, then, must sift further through that Old Testament material to grasp fully what Paul writes. And the Christians of Crete must expect their preacher to wade them through the Old Testament as they take Paul's instruction to heart.

Goal

Paul had a particular goal in mind for the work that he wanted done among the Christians of Crete. Titus must complete the work still unfinished on the island "in hope of eternal life, which God, who never lies, promised before the ages began." The phrase "before the ages began" is a reference to God's decision before he created the world to save particular people ("God's elect") to everlasting life. Notice again that what Paul wrote here is steeped in God's Old Testament revelation. Even as he looked back into history, he also looked forward to what God has planned for the future: eternal life.

Paul, then, had a vision that spans the ages, a vision that is delightful for people habitually stuck in the here and now. Can the God who oversees the ages, however, be trusted? Paul is quick to answer: "God . . . never lies" (v. 2). With those words Paul echoed the words the Holy Spirit caused Balaam to utter to Balak: "God is not a man, that he should lie, or a son of man, that he should change his mind" (Num 23:19). In fact, so faithful is God to his plans from the beginning that he "at the proper time" (v. 3) ensured that his word of life should go to the Gentiles—and for that reason he made Paul his slave and "entrusted" him with the charge to preach his word. As we will see later on, Paul's description of God as one who "never lies" contrasted starkly with what was typical amongst the population of Crete.

Paul, then, had *responsibility* in relation to the elect in Crete (and anywhere else). Yet the Apostle, finite as he was, could not bring the good news to all people by himself alone. That is the reason he instructed Titus to remain on the island of Crete with the assignment to do the work required for these "elect of God" to grow in faith, knowledge, and godliness.

Who is Titus?

Titus, a Greek by birth, accompanied Paul from time to time on his travels (see Gal 2:1; 2 Cor 7:6). It would appear that he had accompanied Paul also to Crete, and was "left" there (1:5) when Paul travelled on.

Of significance for our understanding of this letter is the way Paul described Titus. He called Titus "my true child in a common faith" (v. 4). Paul as the "father" in this relationship had his roots firmly planted in the Old Testament—a revelation that he since his conversion now properly understood. As his "true child," Titus also had appreciation for the Old Testament. The two of them together, father and child, if you will, shared "a common faith" once revealed to generations long promoted to glory. That "common faith" was the motivation propelling Titus to do his task in Crete. Such was the bond between 'father' and 'child' that Paul did not hesitate to declare that "grace and peace from God the Father and Christ Jesus our Savior" were extended to Titus (v. 4). Titus would need this "grace and peace" so very much if he were to accomplish the work Paul assigned him.

Crete

The place where Titus was laboring was the island of Crete, located in the eastern Mediterranean Sea approximately half way between Greece in Europe and Libya in Africa. The island is some 250 kilometers long (from east to west) and varies from ten to fifty kilometers wide (from north to south). The island is mountainous, though some areas are suitable for agriculture. The mountains on the south side of the island tend to drop sheer into the sea, so that the best harbors are found on the north shore. Like the rest of the Mediterranean basin in Paul's day, this island too was part of the Roman Empire.

Very little is known of Paul's connection to Crete. Luke relates that the ship transporting Paul as imperial prisoner to Rome paused at Fair Havens, one of the few harbors on the south shore of Crete (Acts 27:8). That, however, would have been a number of years after Paul wrote his letter to Titus. From Paul's letter to Titus one gets the impression that Paul was less familiar with local details in Crete than he was of other cities to which he had written letters—and that would suggest that he spent little if any time on the island.

Be that as it may, Paul certainly did know what the people of Crete were like. Ever since the fall into sin (Gen 3:6), all people are by nature liars. David put it like this: "Everyone utters lies to his neighbor; with flattering lips and a double heart they speak" (Ps 12:2). Jeremiah added, "The heart is deceitful above all things, and desperately sick" (Jer 17:9). The people of Crete, however, were notorious for their deceit. Paul captured their reputation in Titus 1:12: "One of the Cretans, a prophet of their own, said, 'Cretans are always liars, evil brutes, lazy gluttons.'" The reference is to Epimenides, a Cretan poet and religious reformer who lived some six hundred years before Paul's day. Paul affirmed that "this testimony is true" (1:13). The world of Paul's days had even invented a new word for lying: to *cretize*.

The gospel had come to Crete,[2] and the blessed result was that some on the island were renewed through the Holy Spirit. As a result, the works of the flesh in these people gave way to the fruit of

---

2. We do not know how the gospel arrived in Crete. Perhaps some Cretans who visited Jerusalem at the time of Pentecost took the gospel back with them (Acts 2:11). Perhaps merchants carried the gospel with them as they travelled from the various ports where Paul labored, be it Corinth or Ephesus. It is also possible (though unlikely; see above) that Paul had brought the gospel to the island himself—but there is no record that he ever paid a mission visit to the island. The best we have is that he "left" Titus there (1:5), a detail that indicates that Paul at least touched foot on the island.

the Spirit. Instead of habitually speaking lies, these new believers made it their business to speak truth. Yet given the fact that they were raised to be comfortable with lying, and given the constant deceit they kept hearing around them, plus the inclination to evil that continues to characterize the heart of even the holiest (see Rom 7:13–25), the pressure for these young Christians to give themselves to lying was surely great.

Mandate

With pastoral sensitivity, then, and under the guidance of the Holy Spirit, the Apostle Paul considered what needed to be done among these Cretan Christians. How could church life prosper in a culture of deceit? He "left" Titus in Crete with the mandate to "put what remained into order." That, then, is Titus' specific mandate.

What, however, is meant by the phrase "what remained"?[3] What is the "what" that remained? And what was defective about "what remained" that Titus had to put it in order?

It stands to reason that Titus understood Paul's instruction precisely. He was, after all, Paul's child in a common faith (Titus 1:4). He knew well that Paul was "a servant of God and an apostle of Jesus Christ" (1:1). That standing had given Paul a mandate, as we've drawn out above. Recall: on the road to Damascus the ascended Christ had imposed on Paul the mandate "to carry my name before the Gentiles and kings and the children of Israel" (Acts 9:15). With those words the Lord Jesus Christ had charged Paul with the same mandate he had given to the eleven remaining disciples, "Go therefore and make disciples of all nations, baptizing them into the name of the Father and of the Son and of the Holy Spirit, teaching them to observe all that I have commanded you" (Matt 28:19, 20). According to this mandate the job was not

---

3. For the good flow of the sentence, a word needs to be assumed here describing the notion of unfinished or incomplete or broken. The NKJV adds the word "what is lacking," the KJV has "the things that are wanting," the NIV has "what was left unfinished," the RSV has "what was defective." The NASB translates literally: "what remains," as does the ESV: "what remained."

finished when heathens came to faith so that they were baptized; it was equally important to teach them all things the Lord has commanded. Titus surely knew well that when Paul bade farewell to the elders of Ephesus he reminded them that he "did not shrink from declaring to you anything that was profitable" (Acts 20:20), and described that body of material as "the whole counsel of God" (20:27).[4] He knew: to teach *all* that Jesus Christ commanded is a broad mandate indeed!

Paul now "left" Titus on the island of Crete because the Lord's instruction to teach all that he had commanded had not been completed for the benefit of the Cretan Christians. Titus, then, must set in order what is unfinished, and so give further apostolic, biblical instruction on particular matters as they pertained to the needs of Crete.

From the rest of his letter to Titus it is clear that Paul has two particular matters in mind that need Titus' specific attention. First is the need to "appoint elders in every town" (1:5); Paul details this instruction in the remainder of Titus 1. Second is the need to "teach what accords with sound doctrine" (2:1); this instruction is drawn out in Titus 2 and 3.

POINTS FOR DISCUSSION

1. With the assistance of a Bible dictionary or encyclopedia, dig up what information you can about Paul's youth, education, and zeal for God before his conversion on the road to Damascus. As to his life after his conversion, from the same sources prepare a timeline indicating his missionary journeys. Where does his letter to Titus fit into that timeline?

4. As one reads through Paul's various letters one gets a sense of how wide a range of topics Paul addressed in his preaching and teaching; he certainly did not limit himself to a very narrow agenda of teaching nothing more than Christ crucified, as if that is all that Christians needed to know and believe. During his time in Thessalonica, for example, he spoke candidly about matters of sexuality (1 Thess 4:6) and the expectation of Christ's return (2 Thess 2:5), while with the Philippians he taught about matters of food and drink (Phil 3:18).

2. Paul considered himself a "servant" of God, or, as the word can also be translated, a "slave" of God. In your opinion, is that standing a positive thing or a negative thing? Would you call yourself a slave of God? Why or why not? What consequence follows?

3. Paul calls himself an "apostle" of Jesus Christ. Who were the other apostles? Was Paul called to the apostleship in the same way the other apostles were? If not, what was the difference? Did his mandate differ from that of the other apostles? If so, how?

4. Paul says in v. 2 that "God . . . never lies." Trace the theme of God's truthfulness through the Old Testament. How did this divine characteristic affect what the prophets said? What Jesus said? And what Paul says?

5. Follow the thread of "lying" through the Scriptures. Where does lying come from? How does the prevalence of lying affect relations between people

   a. In the Old Testament?

   b. In Jesus' day?

   c. Today?

6. Do a study to find out what you can learn about Titus. What was his task on the island of Crete? Where would he have received his theological education?

7. Do a study also on what you can learn about Crete. Try to get a handle on what Cretan culture was like. How was it different/similar to your culture today? Would you consider it fertile ground for the gospel? Explain your answer.

8. Have a preliminary round on the two instructions Paul gives to Titus.

   a. Would you think elders in every town are important? Why or why not?

   b. What does the phrase "sound doctrine" make you think of? Would you look forward to receiving "teaching" in "sound doctrine"? Why or why not?

Instruction One

Chapter 3

Appoint Elders in Every Town

PAUL'S FIRST INSTRUCTION TO Titus, caught in 1:5–16, reads as follows:

> This is why I left you in Crete, so that you might put what remained into order, and appoint elders in every town as I directed you— 6 if anyone is above reproach, the husband of one wife, and his children are believers and not open to the charge of debauchery or insubordination. 7 For an overseer, as God's steward, must be above reproach. He must not be arrogant or quick-tempered or a drunkard or violent or greedy for gain, 8 but hospitable, a lover of good, self-controlled, upright, holy, and disciplined. 9 He must hold firm to the trustworthy word as taught, so that he may be able to give instruction in sound doctrine and also to rebuke those who contradict it.

10 For there are many who are insubordinate, empty talkers and deceivers, especially those of the circumcision party. 11 They must be silenced, since they are upsetting whole families by teaching for shameful gain what they ought not to teach. 12 One of the Cretans, a prophet of their own, said, "Cretans are always liars, evil beasts, lazy gluttons." 13 This testimony is true. Therefore rebuke them sharply, that they may be sound in the faith, 14 not devoting themselves to Jewish myths and the commands of people who turn away from the truth. 15 To the pure, all things are pure, but to the defiled and unbelieving, nothing is pure; but both their minds and their consciences are defiled. 16 They profess to know God, but they deny him by their works. They are detestable, disobedient, unfit for any good work.

Note: excellent material has been written over the years about the qualification and work of elders,[1] so that I need not repeat here all that could be said in relation to Paul's instruction to Titus about appointing elders. In what follows I limit myself to the chosen theme of this publication: how appointing elders in every town contributes to finishing Jesus' mandate to Paul.

Titus must appoint elders in every town. The form Paul uses for the verb "appoint" makes clear that the Apostle is thinking of a one-time action on Titus' part, an action he can complete in (relatively) short order. This contrasts with the form of the verbs characterizing the second instruction Titus receives. The verbs "teach" in 2:1, "declare," "exhort" and "rebuke" in 2:15, "remind" in 3:1, and "insist" in 3:8 are all in the present tense, indicating ongoing action. While the first mandate could, presumably, be quickly

1. A small selection: Michael Brown, ed., *Called to Serve: Essays for Elders and Deacons*, Grandville: Reformed Fellowship, 2006; John R. Sittema, *With a Shepherd's Heart: Reclaiming the Pastoral Office of Elder*, Grandville: Reformed Fellowship, 1996; Alexander Strauch, *Biblical Eldership: An Urgent Call to Restore Biblical Church Leadership*, Littleton: Lewis & Roth, 1995; Cornelis van Dam, *The Elder: Today's Ministry Rooted in All of Scripture*, Phillipsburg: P&R, 2009; Timothy Z. Witmer, *The Shepherd Leader: Achieving Effective Shepherding in Your Church*, Phillipsburg: P&R, 2010.

completed, Titus would need to devote himself at length to the second. For now we need to understand the significance of the first instruction.

Why must Titus appoint elders, let alone appoint elders in every town? We realize that appointing elders places a layer of men holding responsibility between Titus and the Christians of each local church. Is that necessary? Did Paul perhaps think Titus was somehow incompetent—so that had Titus been a more competent man there would be no need for elders? Or might it be that Paul considered the Christians of Crete insufficiently mature in Christ so that they needed multiple supervisors over them?

Paul, as we noted before, is thoroughly schooled in the Old Testament. Indeed, as "servant of God and an apostle of Jesus Christ" (1:1), Paul's instruction to Titus is rooted in God's earlier revelation. We need, then, to investigate what the Lord God had revealed in relation to elders. We shall also need to consider what qualifications ought, by God's ordinance, to characterize the men that God would use to govern his church.

Background to Elders

Though fully sufficient in himself to shepherd each of his sheep directly, it has pleased the great Shepherd (Ps 23:1) to look after his sheep by means of (shall we say) "under-shepherds." God ordained a family structure wherein father (and mother) received authority over the children entrusted to his care, and he has the responsibility to image to his children what the care of their heavenly Father and Shepherd looks like (see Gen 18:19; Exod 20:12).

As the family grows to include multiple generations, the role of the father morphs into that of a patriarch. As family heads, the patriarchs Abraham, Isaac, and Jacob provided leadership to the generations in their charge, and made decisions for them. Yet it is also clear that a layer of authority and initiative existed between the patriarch and the people of his clan. Simeon and Levi, for example, thought for themselves when they attacked and destroyed the men of Shechem (Gen 34:25–31).

Moses' Day

When the people of Israel became slaves in Egypt, their bondage no longer allowed for an authoritative patriarch or king. Yet there remained particular men to whom the people looked for leadership and direction. So God told Moses to "go and gather the elders of Israel together" (Exod 3:16) and tell them of God's plan to deliver his people from their bondage. The elders in turn would speak to the people, and would represent them in providing a response. The people themselves did not make decisions (say, by majority vote), but the elders made decisions on behalf of the people (Exod 19:7, 8).

Of course, when God poured his plagues on Egypt, and opened up the Red Sea to lead his people out, he demonstrated that *he* was Israel's leader and Shepherd. At the same time he led his people through the man Moses. Yet as the months of Israel's journey through the desert went by, the Lord made plain that he did not wish his people to have one single human leader who made all the decisions for the people on his own. Instead, he gave to Moses a body of seventy elders to assist him in governing the people (Num 11:16–25). These men were chosen from a much larger body of acknowledged "elders of the people" (Num 11:16), but these seventy would now receive the Holy Spirit so that they could carry out more effectively the duties of leadership the Lord would lay on them.

By the time the people were ready to enter the Promised Land, the body of elders had such authority and esteem in Israel that they gave instructions along with Moses. With the covenant renewal at Mt. Ebal, "Moses and the elders of Israel commanded the people, saying, 'Keep the whole commandment that I command you today'" (Deut 27:1). Similarly, Moses gave the completed law not just to the priests (who carried the ark in which the law was deposited) but also "to all the elders of Israel" (Deut 31:9). The elders were (jointly with the priests) commanded to "read this law before all Israel in their hearing" every seven years (Deut 31:11). As part of their charge to give leadership to the people, they were also to explain Israel's history and God's deeds to the people (Deut 32:7). The fact that "Israel served the Lord all the days of Joshua, and all the days of the elders who outlived Joshua and had known all the work that the Lord did for Israel" (Josh 24:31; cf. Judg 2:7) illustrates the elders' influence within Israel at the time. Their task, then, was ultimately to shepherd the people in the way the Lord would shepherd them, giving wise leadership and sound counsel.

Jesus' Day

In the course of his earthly ministry, the Savior gathered a body of followers around him. Yet he took care to equip a limited number, twelve disciples, to act as leaders among his followers (Mark 3:13–19). He taught them the principles of the kingdom of heaven, sent them out to preach and teach, and even told them that their decisions on earth would affect eternity (Matt 18:18; John 20:23).

The Early Church

In line with the dots distilled from the Old Testament and from the work of the Lord Jesus Christ, the New Testament church understood (under the inspired guidance of the Head of the church) that God's people still needed local leadership. So the church in Jerusalem received guidance not just from the apostles, but also from a body of elders (Acts 15:2,4). Similarly, the Apostle Paul, after he had preached the gospel among the heathen of Asia Minor, "appointed elders for [the converts] in every church" (Acts 14:23). These elders, like the Old Testament elders who had gone before them, were to give leadership and care befitting their role as under-shepherds of the Good Shepherd (1 Peter 5:1–4).

It is then no surprise to read that as Paul sought to instruct Titus on what to do to complete the work that needed to be done among the churches in Crete, he gave first an instruction to appoint elders in every town. The instruction to appoint elders in every church is the necessary lesson flowing from God's earlier revelation and is part of Jesus' instruction to teach *all* that he had commanded.

Decentralized

That *every* town should receive elders also follows from God's earlier revelation. When God delivered his chosen people from their slavery in Egypt, the people had one acknowledged leader in the person of Moses (be it with the assistance of his brother Aaron as mouthpiece, cf. Exod 4:15, 16). The one man Moses, however, simply could not supply all the spiritual guidance the people of Israel required. Hence the advice of his father-in-law to appoint "able men from all the people, men who fear God, who are trustworthy and hate a bribe, and place such men over the people as chiefs of thousands, of hundreds, of fifties, and of tens" (Exod 18:21). Moses followed this sage advice, and set up within Israel a decentralized system of authority and oversight. That a decentralized structure was in fact the will of the Lord was confirmed forty years later when the Holy Spirit moved Moses to instruct Israel (just before they crossed the Jordan to enter the Promised Land): "You shall appoint judges and officers in all your towns that the Lord your God is giving to you, according to your tribes" (Deut 16:18).

When Moses died, Joshua became Israel's leader. Under his leadership the Land of Promise was captured, the people settled in their towns, and presumably judges and officers were appointed in every town. After Joshua's death, no new single leader was appointed to replace him. God himself was Israel's Master, and he was pleased to rule his people through local officials. When the people years later insisted on centralized authority in the person of a king, the Lord explained to Samuel that the people had in fact rejected him as king (1 Sam 8:7). In step with earlier revelation, godly king Jehoshaphat "appointed judges in the land in all the fortified cities of Judah, city by city" (2 Chr 19:5)—and therein took steps again to decentralize leadership.

On the basis of Old Testament passages as these, it follows that Titus was to "appoint elders *in every town*" (that is, in every town where there were Christians).

We appreciate the wisdom of this instruction. We well realize that local leaders have much better contact with the sheep of the Lord's flock than persons living in a distant suburb—let alone in a far away city. There is a reason why the apostles elsewhere call the elders "shepherds" over particular flocks (Acts 20:28; 1 Pet 5:2). For right governing of the church, the Lord required local elders.

Qualifications

What kind of men would the Lord God use to run his church well? Need these men satisfy any criteria? Will any local Cretan chief do, provided he profess the faith?

Instruction from God's earlier revelation again supplies an answer. The people with whom the Lord established his covenant at Mt. Sinai, and in whose midst he was pleased to dwell, were required to be "holy" on grounds that the Lord is holy (Lev 19:2). The point of the term "holy" was that God saw the people of Israel as *different* from the nations around them, and so Israel was to make a point of *being different*. The Israelites were, then, not to *absorb* the unbelieving culture in which they lived, nor were they simply to steer clear of society's worst offences. Rather, God wanted his people to be *distinct* from the world in which they lived, and to show that distinction through a lifestyle of grateful obedience to his good commands.

In keeping with this Old Testament ethic, Paul understood that the church in Crete needed elders who were noticeably different from their fellow islanders. That is why Paul specified that potential elders needed to meet specific qualifications.

Characteristics

Paul had agreed with the Cretan prophet Epimenides that "Cretans are always liars, evil beasts, lazy gluttons" (Titus 1:12). Even Christians were not fully above this sordid reputation, as Paul further made clear: "there are many who are insubordinate, empty talkers and deceivers" (1:10), who through their drivel "are upsetting whole families by teaching . . . what they ought not to teach"—and doing it "for shameful gain." They professed to know God (1:16), perhaps even confessed that Christ was crucified for sinners, and habitually joined the saints in going to church. But they were not above reproach. As their children saw through their hypocrisy, "whole families" were upset (1:11). That makes the question pressing: which (Christian) Cretan, then, should Titus appoint to the office of elder? Paul stipulated specific criteria.

First—Lifestyle

The sort of men Titus should appoint to the office of elder had to be "above reproach" (v. 6), blameless, without fault. The point of the term is not that one is perfect; after all, every Christian (including Paul himself) is "sold under sin" so that "I have the desire to do what is right, but not the ability to carry it out" (Rom 7:14, 18). Paul's point is rather that one's reputation in the community is to be free of guilt. Though dirt be thrown at the (candidate) elder, no dirt will stick in the mind of the public because he is seen as being "above reproach." In the context, that is first of all a reference to being truthful, not lying. After all, the renewing work of the Holy Spirit is such that the Christian Cretan is *changed*, and so is a liar no longer (see 1 Cor 6:9–11).

This blamelessness comes out in two specific details:

- This person is the husband of one wife, literally a one-woman man. He is faithful to her in good days and bad, in health and sickness, in riches and poverty—and seen to be so. So there is no suspicion in the mind of the public that he would cheat on his wife. We note that this sort of behavior contrasts markedly with typical Cretan culture.

- His children are (as we should translate) "faithful." The reference is not to whether his children have embraced the faith (that can be outside the father's control), but whether they have learned to submit to his authority as God's appointed family head. That is something God mandated him to teach his children since infancy, and mandated him also to reinforce while his children were growing up (see Titus 2:2). Children have an uncanny ability to pick out hypocrisy, and if they sense that their father is somehow two-faced in his parenting or in his Christian confession, they may very well respond by giving themselves to a lifestyle of "debauchery or insubordination." Such a lifestyle on the children's part, then, could reflect negatively on their father's genuineness. In the Cretan culture of the day (and also of any day and culture), a lack of genuineness would undermine his effectiveness.

That Paul considers the testimony of these families to be vitally important is evident from the fact that Paul repeats the term "above reproach" in 1:7—and actually does so in strengthened form: "an overseer, as God's steward, *must* be above reproach." The term translated as "must" conveys the notion of necessity on grounds that it is God's revealed will. Jethro had recommended that Moses appoint "men who fear God, who are trustworthy and hate a bribe" (Exod 18:21) and God had decreed that "judges and officers" were to "judge the people with righteous judgment" (Deut 16:18–20). Jesus insisted on the same: "whoever would be great among you must be your servant, and whoever would be first among you must be your slave, even as the Son of Man came not to be served but to serve, and to give his life as a ransom for many" (Matt 20:26–28).

Many of the Cretan Christians, then, did not qualify for the office of elder. Among the Christians of the island, Paul wrote, were "many who are insubordinate, empty talkers and deceivers, especially those of the circumcision party" (1:10). These men were obviously *not* above reproach, and so Titus was not to appoint any of these "many" to the office of elder. Instead, to curb and correct any of these "many," Titus needed to search for men who feared God, who imaged the self-emptying of the Savior, and so were "above reproach." Such men had the moral right to speak on behalf of the Savior.

This material raises, in relation to ourselves, this question: as the local community observes me (assuming I am an elder or am nominated for the office), do they qualify me as "above reproach"? If not, if public opinion thinks mud will stick to me, I simply do not qualify for the office of elder.

Further—Lifestyle

Beyond these two evidences to a candidate's blamelessness, the Apostle lists five characteristics not to be found in any candidate for the office of elder on the island of Crete. "He must not be arrogant or quick-tempered or a drunkard or violent or greedy for gain" (1:7b). Each of those characteristics echoes the works of the flesh mentioned in Galatians 5:19–21, where *self* (and hence one's own wants) is what drives you. Paul mentions these particular vices undoubtedly as a direct reflection on the sort of behavior that characterized the average Cretan: "always liars, evil beasts, lazy gluttons" (1:12).

- The term "arrogant," or overbearing, describes a basic self-ishness that prompts one to ride roughshod over another. An elder was definitely not to share this characteristic lest he be indistinguishable from typical Cretan styles of behavior (1:12; 3:9), and hence be ineffective in shepherding the Lord's church.

- A "quick-tempered" man did not reflect God's patience for and mercy to sinners—and so such a man could not serve as a fitting under-shepherd to the Good Shepherd. In contrast with Christians who were full of self and their own programs (1:12; 3:9), this was obviously another characteristic never to be found in those entrusted with leading the churches on the island.

- A "drunkard" did not exercise the self-control that an elder must display (1:8). On an island characterized by "gluttons" (1:12)—and even Christians continued to share that vice (2:3)—an elder known as a drunkard could clearly not work effectively. God had created people to rule over creation (Gen 1:28); he did not intend creation to rule over people.

- The term "violent" may or may not describe the consequence of excessive drinking. In any case, Paul's description of Cretans as "evil beasts" (1:12) certainly catches the notion of violence; wild animals can be unpredictable and certainly violent when cornered. Elders needed to "rebuke" those who erred (1:9, 13). A sinner cornered in his wrong can react with hostility to a reprimand. An elder, obviously, must never respond in kind, and so Paul insists that the men Titus appoints to the office must "not be . . . violent."

- Finally, an elder "must not be . . . greedy for gain." That Paul would mention this item in the context of his instruction to Titus is again understandable, because of the attitudes so prevalent among the islanders. In fact, "many" of those who had responded to the proclamation of the gospel (1:10) continued to be driven by a spirit of selfish greed. Particularly those Christians of Jewish origin (1:10b) were "empty talkers and deceivers" who were "upsetting whole families by teaching for shameful gain what they ought not to teach" (1:11). These Christians were full of themselves, confident that they knew God well (1:16), and trying to impose their values and thought patterns on whole families, somehow to gain financial or social or psychological advantage for themselves. Such an attitude is not of the Spirit, and so the elder who must "rebuke" these people could not be motivated by personal gain.

We understand that a person reflecting these vices was obviously not renewed by the Holy Spirit, and so was not able to image the Good Shepherd (Gen 1:26–28). As a result, such a person could not lead God's people in holiness. The line flowing through these dots leads us to conclude that the qualifications Paul specifies for Crete remain valid for all times and places.

After the five negatives, Paul mentions six positives. The candidate elder in Crete must be "hospitable, a lover of good, self-controlled, upright, holy, and disciplined" (1:8).

- The term "hospitable" describes the notion of being open to helping strangers, even to the point of opening one's house to them. Paul provides an example of what this hospitality must look like when he later instructs Titus to "do your best to speed Zenas the lawyer and Apollos on their way; see that they lack nothing" (3:13). God's own hospitality to Egyptian slaves in opening the land of Canaan to them provides an example of what God's people are to do for others (Lev 25:35–38).

- A "lover of good" describes a broader level of charity than the term "hospitality," inasmuch as it reaches across the whole board of life. As good is "good" to all (Ps 145:9; Matt 5:44, 45), so the candidate elder must love the "good"—including doing the good—as an opportunity presents itself in all of life.

- The term "self-controlled" describes here a discipline the candidate elder can extend over himself such that he is not overrun by emotion or impulse. He is able instead to think through what needs to happen, and in the process take seriously the reality of Jesus' victory on the cross. In Titus 2:2 Paul requires that all older men are to reflect this same characteristic.

- A man who is "upright" has a reputation in the community that contrasts with the deceit characteristic of the Cretans. He is a man who does what is right by the acceptable standards of the community in general and of Scripture specifically.

- He is also "holy," distinct from the habits of the community, so that he stands out as different, separate, unique. The herd mentality prompts one to frown on being different, but this man who is "holy" stands above this popular social standard.

- The last word Paul mentions is "disciplined," a word that speaks of inner strength. The candidate elder is to have himself in such check that he is known to be virtuous.

We hear in these characteristics an obvious echo of the work of the Spirit in one's heart (see Gal 5:22, 23). These qualities reflect the sort of man that Jesus was in the years of his earthly sojourn. Any person who would address the "insubordinate, empty talkers and deceivers" currently in the church must share the qualities of the Man whose cause they promote. It gets to the heart of being "above reproach," for his lifestyle is "true" to his stated confession—and so gives to those in his charge the example they are to follow. Any elder seeking to be effective in God's church must satisfy these criteria.

Then—Doctrine

Yet it is not simply the brother's lifestyle that is so important. Paul adds that "he must hold firm to the trustworthy word as taught" (1:9). The point is not that every elder in Crete (and elsewhere, for that matter) was to have a Master's degree in theology. The fine point here is rather that a candidate for the office of elder needs first of all to appreciate biblical doctrine so highly that he wants to learn and embrace all that is taught—even if he does not grasp all the intricacies. Of course, a willingness to learn means that he makes a point of learning—and so being willfully ignorant of doctrine disqualifies one from the office.

Again, the Scriptures Paul had are replete with examples of people who made it their business to know God's revealed will, and so adopted an attitude of humility as they pursued deeper insights. This is the sort of man Solomon counseled his sons to be (Prov 9:10; 18:15). Jesus expected his disciples to learn what he taught them.

Lifestyle and doctrine: the two are of one piece. Getting doctrine right is the first step to getting life right—and it is *lifestyle* that illustrates that one has the foundations right. Saying one is a

Christian while at the same time embracing any aspect of Cretan lifestyle (be it lying, dishonesty, hypocrisy—also about the faith!) disqualifies that person from office. In a word, to be (accepted as) an elder amongst Cretans-who-lie, congregation and community alike needed to see the candidate as above reproach, genuine, tolerating no lie in any aspect of life. How else could one credibly "be able to give instruction in sound doctrine and also . . . rebuke those who contradict it" (1:9)!

Rebuke

The Apostle had instructed Titus to "rebuke" those Christians on the island who held to typical Cretan behavior (1:13)—or, as the Greek has it, to *expose* them. But given the prevalence of deceit in Cretan culture, this task was far more than Titus could accomplish by himself. That is why Paul had Titus first appoint elders. Over against deceptive leaders Paul wants several godly elders, men "above reproach" who are able "to give instruction in sound doctrine and also to rebuke those who contradict it" (1:9). These elders, then, would stand with Titus in rebuking the hypocrites in an effort to make them "sound in the faith" (1:13). Their empty talk and deception (1:10) had made whole families spiritually sick, and so concrete work was required to return them again to good spiritual health. At the heart of that work was the instruction to "rebuke them sharply." The wrongs contaminating the faith of whole families had to be rooted out and the errors corrected.

Paul wanted Titus to set in order what was yet incomplete in Crete. *Everything* that God had commanded and revealed in Old Testament Scripture and in the words and works of Jesus Christ needed to be instilled upon the Christians of the island. Part of that instruction included the appointment of elders, men who could in turn contribute to teaching more of God's glorious revelation.

How delightful: local men functioning in the biblical office of elders are God's tools of choice to tackle the root problem of the island's culture! Titus must finish what is incomplete—appoint elders—so that the work of Jesus Christ in Crete might advance. What glorious vision for the island!

<hr>

POINTS FOR DISCUSSION

1. Does your church have elders? Why or why not? Trace through the Scriptures what the Lord's will might be in relation to whether a church should have elders.

2. If yes, describe the role you understand your body of elders to have in the church. Then go through the Scriptures to glean from them what the Lord's mandate to elders might be.

3. To your understanding, are your elders accountable to the members of the congregation? Should they be? Explain your answer with reference to the Bible.

4. In your judgment, does your body of elders measure up to the qualifications the Apostle mentions to Titus? If needed, what can be done to improve their qualifications?

5. The Lord's church will need elders to shepherd our children in twenty or thirty years' time. What is your church doing today to ensure that there will be sufficient well-equipped elders in time to come? What could you personally do to ensure that there will sufficient elders?

6. What does Paul mean with the requirement that elders must be "above reproach"? Why would this qualification be so important in the Cretan context? How important is this qualification in your community? Are there other qualifications you think your elders ought to have in order to be effective in your specific community? Why would you list these? Are they scripturally justified?

7. Evaluate the claim that getting doctrine right is the first step to getting life right. How important is precise doctrine in your community? Is there a danger in laying too much emphasis on right doctrine? Explain your answer.

Instruction Two

Chapter 4

Teach Sound Doctrine

PAUL'S INTENT WAS THAT Titus should complete what was yet lacking among the churches of Crete. To achieve that goal, Paul wanted Titus to ordain in every town locals who had the qualifications to be elders. We appreciate that a body of elders in each town can accomplish so very much more in caring for the church than Titus was able to accomplish on his own. So we somehow expect that with the appointment of elders Titus has completed all that needs to be done for the Christians of Crete.

That conclusion would not be correct. Even a body of elders cannot do all the work that needs to happen within a given congregation. In fact, the Lord God has revealed that every saint needs to be conscripted for service. How, though, is Titus to recruit the saints? This is the topic of the second section of Paul's letter to Titus (Titus 2:1—3:11).

> 2 But as for you, teach what accords with sound doctrine.
> 2 Older men are to be sober-minded, dignified, self-controlled, sound in faith, in love, and in steadfastness.
> 3 Older women likewise are to be reverent in behavior, not slanderers or slaves to much wine. They are to teach what is good, 4 and so train the young women to love their husbands and children, 5 to be self-controlled, pure, working at home, kind, and submissive to their

own husbands, that the word of God may not be reviled. 6 Likewise, urge the younger men to be self-controlled. 7 Show yourself in all respects to be a model of good works, and in your teaching show integrity, dignity, 8 and sound speech that cannot be condemned, so that an opponent may be put to shame, having nothing evil to say about us. 9 Bondservants are to be submissive to their own masters in everything; they are to be well-pleasing, not argumentative, 10 not pilfering, but showing all good faith, so that in everything they may adorn the doctrine of God our Savior.

11 For the grace of God has appeared, bringing salvation for all people, 12 training us to renounce ungodliness and worldly passions, and to live self-controlled, upright, and godly lives in the present age, 13 waiting for our blessed hope, the appearing of the glory of our great God and Savior Jesus Christ, 14 who gave himself for us to redeem us from all lawlessness and to purify for himself a people for his own possession who are zealous for good works.

15 Declare these things; exhort and rebuke with all authority. Let no one disregard you.

3 Remind them to be submissive to rulers and authorities, to be obedient, to be ready for every good work, 2 to speak evil of no one, to avoid quarreling, to be gentle, and to show perfect courtesy toward all people. 3 For we ourselves were once foolish, disobedient, led astray, slaves to various passions and pleasures, passing our days in malice and envy, hated by others and hating one another. 4 But when the goodness and loving kindness of God our Savior appeared, 5 he saved us, not because of works done by us in righteousness, but according to his own mercy, by the washing of regeneration and renewal of the Holy Spirit, 6 whom he poured out on us richly through Jesus Christ our Savior, 7 so that being justified by his grace we might become heirs according to the hope of eternal life. 8 The saying is trustworthy, and I want you to insist on these things, so that those who have believed in God may be careful to devote themselves to good works. These things are excellent and profitable for

people. 9 But avoid foolish controversies, genealogies, dissensions, and quarrels about the law, for they are unprofitable and worthless. 10 As for a person who stirs up division, after warning him once and then twice, have nothing more to do with him, 11 knowing that such a person is warped and sinful; he is self-condemned.

Titus must "teach what accords with sound doctrine" (2:1). Each person in the congregation needs "sound doctrine," and so Titus is instructed to address successively the older men of the churches with respect to their responsibilities (2:2), the older women in relation to theirs (2:3, 4), the young women (2:4, 5), the younger men (2:6–8), and the slaves (2:9, 10)—and do it all in step with the revelation God had earlier given in the Old Testament and through the earthly ministry of the Lord Jesus Christ. The catalyst driving proper conduct in these respective groups is the appearing of the grace of God in Jesus Christ (2:11–14). Just how adamant Paul is that Titus teach this material is underlined in 2:15: "declare these things; exhort and rebuke with all authority. Let no one disregard you." In fact, Titus is to "insist on these things" (3:8), so much so that nothing is to distract Titus from this task, certainly not the "foolish controversies" that obsess so many people's minds (3:9).

In chapter 2 Paul develops members' responsibility toward those *inside* the church (i.e., each is to pay attention to the other, in the awareness that outsiders are watching). In 3:1–8 the Apostle draws out the responsibility members have with respect to those *outside* the church—again in the awareness that outsiders are always watching. Society, after all, "reads" church members to determine whether the gospel is worth considering. To change the apostate culture of Crete, Paul would have Titus harness the resources of each Christian on the island, regardless of age or social status.

In fulfilling such a demanding assignment Titus is to ensure that he is not distracted from his preaching and teaching (3:9–11).

1. Titus must teach what accords with "sound doctrine."

   a. Put into words what you expect the phrase "sound doctrine" to mean.

   b. Where is Titus to get this "sound doctrine" from?

   c. Would you imagine the Christians of Crete to be keen to hear "sound doctrine"? Are people in your church keen to hear it? Are you? If not, why not?

2. God's people never live in a vacuum, but always rub shoulders with those around us. How do those around you gain a handle on what you actually believe?

3. Titus is told to "teach," with parallel words used in 2:15 ("exhort" and "rebuke"), 3:1 ("remind") and 3:8 ("insist"). In church services today, emphasis tends to lie on "worship" and "praise."

   a. Why would our day lay emphasis on "worship" in favor of "teach"?

   b. Is this a good emphasis? Why or why not?

Chapter 5

Older Men

THE APOSTLE PAUL HAS mandated Titus to set in order particular matters still incomplete in the churches of Crete. To the Apostle's mind, mobilizing the older men is essential for the well being of the churches, and so they are to receive Titus' attention first (2:1, 2). Concerning these older men, Paul gives this instruction to Titus:

> 1 But as for you, teach what accords with sound doctrine.
> 2 Older men are to be sober-minded, dignified, self-controlled, sound in faith, in love, and in steadfastness.

As we seek to unpack what the Apostle wants Titus to teach older men, we need to turn first to the Old Testament, where God first revealed "sound doctrine," and through which God schooled his servant Paul. We then turn to consider what this "sound doctrine" means for the older men in Crete before we draw out some consequences for ourselves.

The Old Testament: The Place of the Man

Men Are Not Women

God created the human race, male and female, to image what God is like. Man and woman would image God through the way in which they would rule over God's world (Gen 1:26). God did not, however, create the two genders at the same time. He first made a man, placed him in the garden, and gave him alone the command to work it and take care of it (Gen 2:15). The man was, in other words, responsible to take initiative in fulfilling his duties before God.

The Lord saw that it was not good for the man to be alone, and so made a "helper" for him (2:18). In the relation between the man and the woman in Paradise, *he* was the leader and she was not; *she* was the helper and he was not. So when God came to the Adam and Eve after their fall into sin, he sought out the *man*: "where are you?" (3:9). He faulted Adam for two transgressions; the first is "you have listened to the voice of your wife," and the second is "[you] have eaten of the tree" (3:17). In describing the first transgression as he did, the Lord underlined that Adam was responsible to give leadership and so was to disagree with his wife's course of action in reaching for the forbidden fruit. His penalty includes that the Savior will come through "her offspring," not his (3:15).

Subsequent chapters of divine revelation illustrate the leadership role God assigned to the man:

- Only masculine names are listed in the genealogies of Genesis 5 and 10. Obviously women are implied in the lists, but the families are named from the men, not from the women.

- The Lord did not call Sarai to take her husband and leave her mother's household, but summoned Abram to take his wife and leave his father's household (Gen 12:1).

- The sign almighty God ordained for the covenant (circumcision) was to be given to boys alone (Gen 17:10, 11). Girls were certainly included in God's covenant of love with sinners, but it was the (potential) family head who had to carry the sign of God's covenant.

- At Mt. Sinai the Lord God appointed only men to be elders among the people and to serve in the priesthood (Exod 18:21, 25; 28:1).

- God gave his covenant law at Mt. Sinai to all the people, regardless of age, gender or social status. Yet he obviously addressed his people through the men, for he told the crowds they were "not [to]covet your neighbor's wife" (Exod 20:17).

- God required that the males of Israel were to appear before the Lord three times a year (Exod 23:17; Deut 16:16).

- The Lord Jesus Christ was born a male (Matt 1:25).

- Jesus appointed twelve disciples to be with him and serve as leaders in the New Testament church. They were all men (Mark 3:16–19).

- After Pentecost the twelve requested the "brothers" of the congregation to "pick out from among you seven men of good repute" (Acts 6:3).

It cannot be said that these items (and so many others) are recorded as they are because of the influence of the culture of the day. The Lord did not hesitate to instruct Israel to stay away from particular practices he condemned among the nations around Israel (see Lev 18). Had he been displeased with the male headship so obviously taught and followed in earlier revelation, he most certainly would have said so explicitly. As it is, each illustration listed above represents another dot through which a line can be drawn from Paradise through to the days of the Apostle Paul in the New Testament dispensation, all consistently making plain that God would have men be the leaders.[1] When Paul, then, tells Titus what to teach the older men, he is deliberately giving instruction about that segment of the human race that is commissioned to take responsibility and give leadership.

---

1. I have elaborated at length on this point in my book *A Vow to Love: A Biblical Explanation of the Form for the Solemnization of Marriage* (Winnipeg: Premier, 2008) 75–89.

Older

The men Titus must teach are "older." The term "older" is relative, of course, and assumes the presence of "younger" people. The word describes those men who have spent more years than their students in the school of life and so are in a position to show the younger how to *do* life. Though Paul used the word to describe himself when he was some sixty years old (Phlm 9), the term denotes anyone who is "older" than another—and so may certainly be used of persons younger than sixty.

Today's Western culture says that "older men" deserve the opportunity to kick back, enjoy life and play with the toys they accumulated through their hard work. Beneath that polite exterior is the thought that the older men are actually out of touch, cannot keep up with the fast pace of the younger, and so are really beyond their use-by date; they should be retired from any role of leadership or influence in society. There is an echo of this thought in the church, to the effect that the older men (are made to) feel passed by and even uncertain about their purpose. The result is that they retreat into their seniors' circle, and become an untapped resource.

Task

This was not the intent of the Lord God. He created the first man (and woman) in his image, and gave the command to "be fruitful and multiply and fill the earth and subdue it and have dominion over the fish of the sea and over the birds of the heavens and over every living thing that moves on the earth" (Gen 1:27, 28). Children born in Paradise, however, would not know by instinct how to rule over God's world in a way that imaged God; the older generation was to teach the younger how to do this. Of course, the longer Adam lived in the school of life, the better he would know what God was like, and so the better equipped he would be to teach coming generations how to "have dominion over" God's creatures in a way pleasing to God. Clearly, as the God-appointed leader, the responsibility to train those after him belonged primarily to Adam.

The fall into sin complicated the task enormously. But it did not change the expectations God had for Adam as he grew older, or for the subsequent generations of older men. So God told Moses that he poured plagues on Egypt "that you may tell in the hearing of your son and of your grandson how I have dealt harshly with the Egyptians . . . that you may know that I am the Lord" (Exod 10:2). Moses, we need to know, was more than eighty years old (see Exod 7:7) at the time God gave him this instruction. Talk about the role of "the older men"! Fully in line with this command is the prayer of the psalmist: "Even to old age and gray hairs, O God, do not forsake me, until I proclaim your might to another generation, your power to all those to come" (Ps 71:18). One never outgrows the mandate to instruct the younger how to handle the hills and valleys of life.

Wisdom

Because of the role God assigned to the aged, the Lord commanded the youth of Israel to respect the seniors (and not just the grandparents); as an older man approached them, the youth were to "stand up" and "honor the face of an old man" (Lev 19:32). Here was recognition that the older have learned so much in God's school-of-life as to be a reservoir of experience and wisdom the younger were to treasure.

Sadly, not all older men speak only wisdom. Job's three senior friends spoke the language of fools in their reprimands to Job (see Job 42:7; 32:6–22). Solomon advised older folk not to wonder, "Why were the former days better than these?" (Eccl 7:10). Young people live in the God-given present (and not in the past), and in the challenges God gives today they need encouragement—not the signal that today is too hard. Older men, in other words, need to make it their business to be careful how they analyze the present in relation to the past; their analysis requires ongoing Bible study and thought so that in turn their instruction to the younger is beneficial.

The New Testament: Characteristics of Older Men

All this Old Testament material came along in Paul's instruction to Titus to "teach what accords with sound doctrine" (Titus 2:1). For the benefit of the churches of Crete, Paul drew out the implication of the role God had assigned to the older men: "older men are to be sober-minded, dignified, self-controlled, sound in faith, in love, and in steadfastness."

Sober-Minded

The term translated as "sober-minded" is often used in relation to drink and so becomes instruction to be moderate in how much you drink. Yet Paul's point is not that older men are simply to exercise moderation in drinking. Rather, in all of life one is to be moderate, not indulgent, not extravagant, not into excess or glut. Herein the "older men" of the church would contrast with the typical attitude of the Cretans around them; they were "always . . . lazy gluttons" (1:12).

What, though, is wrong with excess? Why must Titus make a point of telling older men to be moderate? Older men ought to have learned the truth of Solomon's words in Ecclesiastes 2:1–11, when he tried all sorts of excess in his attempt to make sense of life. As so many young men do in an effort to figure out life, Solomon too sought fulfillment in wine, houses, gardens, women, song, parties, and more. But the more he tried, the more he realized that *things* do not lift us out of the thorns and thistles of a life outside Paradise (Gen 3:18). His conclusion was this: "then I considered all that my hands had done and the toil I had expended in doing it, and behold, all was vanity and a striving after wind" (Eccl 2:11). That was the advantage of older age: Solomon could tell the younger in his realm that he'd been there, done that, and they should take instruction from him and not repeat his futile search.

This is the message Titus was to instruct older men to convey to the younger in Crete. Those older men had been around for many years, and so had tested the value of *more and more stuff*, and were now in a position to vouch for the truth of Ecclesiastes 2. These "older men" have "fought the good fight," have nearly "finished the race" (2 Tim 4:7), and now await the summons of the Lord to enter the presence of their Father through Christ. So their lifestyle was to illustrate that life is not about food, property, good looks, degrees, music, chocolate, gin, women, cars, etc. Instead, their lifestyle should reflect the delightful fact that "the grace of God has appeared, bringing salvation for all people" (Titus 2:11); Christ has come to redeem sinners and take away the *cause* of our eternal hunger and misery. Through his self-emptying on the cross he has in principle restored sinners to Paradise. Since that is so, older men need to be consistent and "renounce ungodliness and worldly passions" (2:12), say "No" to more toys, more drink, more "buzz," etc., and live instead "godly lives in the present age, waiting for our blessed hope, the appearing of the glory of our great God and Savior Jesus Christ" (2:13). Hence a "sober-minded" lifestyle is in place, moderate in one's demand for food and drink, for wealth and holiday. That is the "older men": they have learned through the school of life to get their priorities right, so that their emphasis lies not on *things* but on the great commission given in Paradise. They take responsibility and initiative in serving God and neighbor— and in so doing follow the example of "Jesus Christ, who gave himself for us" (2:14). For the wellbeing of the church, the older men needed deliberately to model the sober-mindedness that comes with embracing the gospel of Jesus Christ.

Dignified

Titus must also instruct "older men" to carry themselves in a dignified manner. Through the course of their lives, these men have faced many trials—burying parents and perhaps a spouse or a child; they have been through sickness, fire, war, flood, drought, and more. In the process they have learned that their heavenly Father uses these challenges to train them for further service and fruitfulness (Heb 12:10, 11; Jas 1:2–4). These older men reflect these hard lessons in their lives as they live seriously, with the question always pressing on their minds: what is God teaching me through this?

This does not make the older men boring or gloomy, as if life for them cannot be enjoyed. On the contrary, these men live in the awareness that God shapes and guides each moment, a reality that brings freedom and makes life exciting and delightful as they see God continuing to lead them and mold them for further service. These older men model this awareness for the benefit of the entire congregation. They are able to encourage, warn and instruct other believers—and that is the sort of leadership all the members of the church need in order to prosper in God's service.

Self-Controlled

Titus must tell "older men" to be disciplined. They, after all, (ought to) have learned how to get the passions and instincts of youth under control. As a result, they act less out of impulse, with decisions more thought through. They have learned to live life sensibly, seriously, and so with fitting restraint.

Healthy

The accumulated effect of being sober-minded, dignified, and self-controlled is good health—a term that comes back in our translation as "sound." Yet the reference is not necessarily to health-of-body but to health-of-spirit, as the Apostle makes plain when he connects a series of words to the term "healthy": "sound in faith, in love and in steadfastness." As a result of the lessons learned over many years in the school of life, older men (are meant to) have become healthy in their faith in God, relying on him in even-keeled manner in the midst of life's storms and challenges. Similarly, they have become healthy in their love for God and therefore for their neighbor, denying self in order to serve the other. Again, older men have learned to be healthy in endurance, not anemic in their determination to fulfill their God-given role in life, but robust—even in old age—in exercising their (remaining) gifts and opportunities to God's glory and the neighbor's benefit. As the psalmist had put it: "The righteous flourish like the palm tree . . . They still bear fruit in old age; they are ever full of sap and green, to declare that the Lord is upright" (Ps 92:12–15).

Nothing New

This, then, is the sound doctrine Titus was to encourage the older men amongst the Christians of Crete to exemplify. As the older men among the Christians did so, their lifestyle would contrast sharply with the excess that Cretans typically celebrated. Recall Paul's summary of what Cretans were like: "Cretans are always liars, evil brutes, lazy gluttons" (Titus 1:12). The Christians of Crete were raised in that culture and, despite their conversion, remained vulnerable to what was accepted around them (Jer 17:9; Rom 7:15, 18). It was tempting for them to revert to the attitude typical of Cretans: "eat, drink, and be merry." One can picture the "older men" amongst the "lazy gluttons" of the island, with their shrunken biceps and ample waistline assembled in the coffee shops, conversing about the latest horse race, hockey game, cruise, property deal, or woman as they slurp their latte.

It snaps Paul's instruction to Titus into sharp focus: these God-ordained leaders are to "be sober-minded, dignified, self-controlled," and so *be examples for the women and younger men to follow*. This, Paul stresses, is imperative if congregational life is to function as God wants it to (1:5a).

Today

The thought is enduring, and relevant for all ages and peoples. The Lord has prepared a glorious future for his (older) children, yet does not take every older brother to glory as soon as he is an empty nester or has reached the age God allotted to man (Ps 90:10). In fact, God never puts older brothers out to pasture, but mandates them to continue to be *examples* to the rest of his people. So, let today's older men take up their God-given task with confidence! The older have spent years in the school of life and so learned that it is not *things* which bring fulfillment, salvation, or purpose; rather, the power of the gospel of Jesus Christ restoring sinners to God is what gives life purpose, significance, and fulfillment. Let older men, then, *model* the gospel for the benefit of the rest of the congregation, and be moderate, dignified, and self-controlled in a manner the younger of the flock can see and admire. Let older men take their mentorship role seriously as long as God gives strength and opportunity. That includes that they seek out the younger in order to speak to them of the works of the Lord as they have experienced them over the years. It is a privileged fact: for the church to function as the Lord desires, *the younger need the leadership, example, and instruction of the older*. That reality is part and parcel of "sound doctrine" as God has revealed it in earlier Scripture and as Jesus Christ commanded his disciples to teach those they have baptized (Matt 28:20).

Preacher

The God who gave the separate dots in Genesis, Exodus, Leviticus, etc., and caused the Apostle to connect the dots to the inevitable instruction of Titus 2:2 does not change (Num 23:19). That is why every preacher throughout the ages, irrespective of culture or context must "declare these things; exhort and rebuke with all authority." That preacher is to let "no one," not even the older men, "disregard you" (2:15)—for the sound doctrine the preacher must proclaim concerning older men comes from God himself.

POINTS FOR DISCUSSION

1. This chapter listed several evidences that the Lord God assigned the leadership role in human society to the man. Evaluate whether the evidences listed are persuasive. On grounds that no list is complete, find further evidences in Scripture to demonstrate the point. Can you also find evidence that the Lord assigned the leadership role in human society to women? Or that God would have men and women both be leaders in equal measure?

2. What is meant by the phrase "older men"? What age group would you think would be addressed in your congregation with this phrase? What expectations do you have of the "older men" of your congregation? Are they being used to the full? If not, how could they be better utilized?

3. Would you consider Eli (1 Sam 1–5) a good model for older men to follow? What does 1 Samuel 4:18 suggest about his eating habits? What does 1 Samuel 2:22–25 indicate about his influence over his sons? What lessons follow?

4. How does the gospel of Christ's victory (see Titus 2:11–14) impact the way older men ought to live?

5. For the older men: are you the sort of men Paul would want you to be? Perhaps ask the younger men, or maybe the older women, whether your age group comes across as "soberminded" or as given to excess, whether your age group has learned much from the school of life or whether your group comes across as flippant or perhaps even irresponsible. Give consideration to what your group could do better to be more effective to the younger in your midst.

6. For the younger: are you open to learning from the older men in your midst, be it through conversation with them, be it through following their example? Do you have any systems in place to connect the older with the younger?

7. Do you experience a generation gap between yourself and these "older men"? In what way is that gap (in part) your

fault? In what ways is it their fault? What can you do to (help) bridge that gap?

8. If you were the (young) preacher in your congregation (as Titus was on the island), how would you go about "teaching" these older men the "sound doctrine" they need to embrace?

9. Elders are commonly busy men. How can your elders mobilize the older men in your midst so that some work is taken off their plate and the congregation is properly shepherded?

Chapter 6

Older Women

THE SECOND GROUP WITHIN the congregation Titus must address is the older women (2:3, 4a). More often than not, there are more senior women in the church of the Lord than senior men. What task would the Lord give these sisters in his church?

> 1 But as for you, teach what accords with sound doctrine . . . 3 Older women likewise are to be reverent in behavior, not slanderers or slaves to much wine. They are to teach what is good, 4 and so train the young women to . . .

The term "older women" directs our thoughts to those sisters who have spent more time than many others have in God's school of life and so have acquired the experience needed to touch others in a helpful manner. We do not know whether the older women Paul was speaking about were married, single, or widowed, but it is surely safe to assume that some were married, while others had never married or were now widowed. In any case, Paul does not speak here about the role of the older women in relation to a husband; he speaks instead about their role as teachers. It is this thread of older women as teachers that we need to trace through God's earlier revelation.

The Foundation: The Task God Gave to the Woman

Teachers

The Lord God in the beginning created two people, a man and a woman, to image him. He gave them the command to "be fruitful and multiply and fill the earth and subdue it and have dominion over" all creatures (Gen 1:28). God's intent was that not just two people image God, but that the earth would be filled with people who reflected what God was like. Yet the children to be born would not know from instinct how to image God; they would need to *be taught*. This was, of course, the parents' task, with Eve as mother to play a central role. The longer Eve spent in the school of life, the better she would get to know God—and so the better equipped she would be to teach those who came after her what service to God ought to look like.

This task would, of course, be true not just for her, but also for her daughters through the generations. The fall into sin complicated the task profoundly, but it did not alter God's intent for the "older women." Always these "older women," made wise by years in God's service, would have a vital role to play for the benefit of the younger.

It is no surprise, then, to find Miriam teaching the women of Israel. Miriam was Moses' older sister (Exod 2:7), and Moses was eighty years old when the Lord sent him to Egypt to deliver his people (Exod 7:7). With the exodus now behind them, the aged Miriam led the women with tambourines and dancing as they sang the Lord's praise on account of his redeeming work (Exod 15:20, 21). Similarly, the "excellent wife" of Proverbs 31 "opens her mouth with wisdom, and the teaching of kindness is on her tongue" (v. 26). Abigail did not hesitate to set David straight (1 Sam 25:18–31), and it is not without significance that Joab used "the woman from Tekoa" to address David about Absalom's exile (2 Sam 14:4). At eighty-four years of age Anna spoke readily of the newborn Savior "to all who were waiting for the redemption of Jerusalem" (Luke 2:36–38).

The Application in Crete: Traits of the Woman

The line Paul drew through these Old Testament dots led him to instruct Titus concerning what the "sound doctrine" he needed to "teach" the older women must look like. "Older women" must "teach what is good"—an instruction fully in line with God's earlier revelation. Yet to be effective in teaching, these older sisters needed to live a life consistent with sound doctrine before they could be expected to influence the younger in a positive manner. So Paul told Titus to ensure that the older women were "to be reverent in behavior, not slanderers or slaves to much wine" (Titus 2:3).

Reverent in Behavior

The term translated as "reverent in behavior" is literally: "in behavior befitting a temple." It is a formulation full of gospel, and hence of grateful obligation.

The Lord God had told his people at Mt. Sinai to build a house for him, where he could live among them. The tabernacle Israel built had the Most Holy Place—where God was enthroned on the ark between the cherubim—in the back, hidden from public eye by the curtain. The people had to stay outside the tabernacle, for God was too holy to have sinners in his immediate presence. Between the people outside and the Lord inside stood the altar for sacrifices. That altar spoke of the work the Mediator Jesus Christ was going to do; he would one day sacrifice himself on the cross to atone for sins so that sinners might be reconciled to God. In its structure, then, the tabernacle illustrated the gospel of grace; Christ was the Mediator between holy God and sinful people.

In the course of years, Christ Jesus actually did come to pay for sin, and triumphed too. As a result, the curtain preventing access to the presence of God in the Most Holy Place was torn (Matt 27:51). After his ascension into heaven, Christ poured out his Holy Spirit so that in him God might dwell in sinners' hearts. The result is that believers are temples of the Holy Spirit (1 Cor 3:16; 6:19).

That was a reality true also for the saints of Crete, including the "older women." That is the force of Titus 2:11: "For the grace of God that brings salvation has appeared to all men."

The implication is clear: if you are a temple, you need to live a lifestyle befitting that status. That is what Paul wants Titus to impress on the "older women"; in step with "sound doctrine" (2:1), they are to *act* as temples of the Holy Spirit. Of course, others of the congregation are to act that way too, but Paul is now concerned specifically that the older women be what they are because God has entrusted a teaching role to them.

Behavior Befitting a Temple

What might a lifestyle "befitting a temple" look like? Here we must refer to Leviticus 10:1–11, a portion of Old Testament Scripture from which Paul drew numerous allusions for his instruction in Titus 2:3.

The book of Leviticus follows the completion of the tabernacle God wanted Israel to build (see Exod 40:33). Leviticus 1–7 detail how the sacrifices on that altar between God and the people were to be performed, while Leviticus 8 explains who had to preside over the sacrifices on that altar. Chapter 9 describes the ordination of the priests, and then ends with Aaron blessing the Israelites and the glory of the Lord appearing to the people. An exciting day: God and sinners could live together in harmony; here something of Paradise was restored!

The sons of Aaron got caught up in the excitement of the moment, says Leviticus 10, and in their enthusiasm volunteered a sacrifice on that altar. Bam! "Fire came out from before the Lord and consumed them, and they died before the Lord" (v. 2). How tragic! But the lesson was so obvious: God is holy. Somehow, spontaneous sacrifice was behavior *not* befitting the temple.

Now that the Holy Spirit has been poured out on Pentecost, the point is even more true for New Testament temples. The "older women," teachers (and hence models) as they are, need to adopt behavior befitting a temple, and so are, in their service to God, to be even more particular and even more careful than the priests of Leviticus 10 (and hence of the Old Testament) had to be. For God remains God!

Paul works out in Titus 2:12 what this looks like. "The grace of God has appeared, bringing salvation for all people," and it trains us "to renounce ungodliness and worldly passions"—including the inner urge to serve God in a self-chosen way. Instead, our identity as "temples" teaches us, Paul continues, "to live self-controlled, upright and godly lives in the present age."

That teaching happens through the example of the older women—and Paul is happy to flesh that out in further detail still.

Not Slanderers

Paul follows the instruction to live in a fashion "befitting a temple" with the command not to be "slanderers." The word translated as "slanderers" is actually the same word that appears repeatedly in the Bible as the name of the Devil: *Diabolos*. In the original Greek, this word describes the notion of sowing confusion, which is exactly what slander does to someone's reputation. It is, therefore, evil and ungodly, and that is why the "older women" of Titus' congregations were studiously to avoid it.

One wonders, though, why Paul felt the need to tell Titus to teach the women not to slander. Were the Cretan ladies excessively guilty of this evil? The fact that "Cretans are always liars, evil brutes, lazy gluttons" (as Paul affirmed in 1:12) leaves room for that understanding. Yet more is involved here.

The Lord God responded to Aaron's sons' spontaneous worship with heavenly fire and death. One could understand very well that Aaron would be tempted to respond to God's deed with serious criticism of God's high standards. Moses, however, reminded Aaron of God's holiness, with the result that "Aaron held his peace" (Lev 10:3). He did not slander God's good name despite the anguish he undoubtedly felt at the death of his sons, nor did he sow confusion among the people about what kind of a God they had. Since God had come to live among the people in the tabernacle, the people needed to conduct themselves as persons "befitting the temple"—and by his remaining silent, not slandering God, Aaron exemplified precisely that sort of behavior.

The "older women" of Crete, now, were to adopt behavior "befitting a temple." An essential aspect of that behavior was that they would not slander God's good name, be it through their own misconduct or by giving someone else occasion to think or speak evil of God. In fact, their words were always to be inspiration for others to think highly of God and of his deeds, and so to praise him.

Not Slaves to Much Wine

Wine (and it is true of all alcoholic drink) is a gift from God. God told Adam and Eve on the day of their creation that "I give you every plant yielding seed that is on the face of all the earth" (Gen 1:29). God also told them that they were to "have dominion" over all creation (Gen 1:28)—and that means that they were to see to it that no created thing ruled over them. To be ruled by alcohol, then, is sin. That is true in terms of addiction, and is true too when one is "under the influence." Hence the Bible's repeated instruction to use wine in moderation (see Prov 23:19–21; 1 Tim 5:23). The older women of Crete were to take this biblical instruction to heart.

Again, though, one wonders why Paul would mention this matter to Titus. Did the older women of Crete have a problem with alcohol? That "Cretans are . . . lazy gluttons" (1:12) could suggest it was so. It is important to note that drinking receives mention in Leviticus 10. After the bodies of Aaron's two dead sons were carried away from the tabernacle, the Lord told Aaron, "Drink no wine or strong drink, you and your sons with you, when you go into the tent of meeting" (v. 9). As the priests labored at the altar in God's presence, they should be clear-headed and in full control of their faculties; God, after all, was holy. Given that the "older women" of Crete—teachers as they were to be—were to behave in a manner befitting temples, it follows that nothing should becloud their judgment; always they should be clear-headed.

Teach What Is Good

One needs good judgment if one is to "teach what is good" and so "train the young women" (2:3, 4). We have already drawn out above that the Lord had assigned a teaching role to the women, with its focus on the coming generations. Strikingly, though, this again is an echo of Leviticus 10. For after the Lord had forbidden Aaron and his sons to drink wine whenever they went into the Tent of Meeting, the Lord added this instruction: "You must distinguish between the holy and the common, and between the unclean and the clean, and you are to teach the people of Israel all the statutes that the Lord has spoken to them by Moses" (Lev 10:10, 11). In subsequent chapters of Leviticus the Lord expanded on the unclean and clean in relation to foods, animals, fish, skin, clothes, houses, and more. The point of the distinctions was that Israel was daily to know that they were different from the nations; they were holy and therefore to tolerate no sin in their lives. This point required teaching, and that task fell to the priests as they labored in the tabernacle—and they, for the sake of teaching clearly, had to be alcohol free. Again, the priests were to "teach the people of Israel all the statutes that the Lord [had] spoken to them by Moses," and that includes instruction about all the main points of doctrine as the Lord taught it through the laws.

This teaching function belonged to the priest. But Paul in Titus 2 refers back to Leviticus 10 to undergird how the "older women" are to teach. Their conduct is to be consistent with the Christians' identity as temples of the Holy Spirit, they are not to slander God's works and words, and they are to be consistently clear-minded as they join Titus in teaching the younger women the implications of the faith.

Let no one misunderstand. Paul is not saying—and I am not either—that the "older women" are to receive a place of leadership in the church. The Holy Spirit moved the Apostle elsewhere to write, "I do not permit a woman to teach or to have authority over a man; she must be silent" (1 Tim 2:12). Yet Paul would not have women pushed into a corner as if they have no role in the congregation! Very deliberately Paul uses language in Titus 2:3 that is borrowed from Leviticus 10:1–11, concerning the priests' role as teachers, and applies that instruction to the older women. As Paul would have Titus teach sound doctrine thus far insufficiently taught in Crete, he would have the older women drawn in to play a vital role! Yet that vital role is not directed to the congregation in its entirety, but is directed to the "younger women" of the flock. These "younger women" also have a critical role to play (see chapter 6 below) but Titus cannot reach them so easily. So, in relation to these younger women, the older have that position of teaching—as a clear echo of God's intent in Genesis 1.

Value

Paul would not have the older women of Crete—or of today—cloistered in some seniors' club, or perhaps forever away on holidays. Sound doctrine implies that the women play a vital role in promoting the health of the congregation. These sisters—they have spent years in God's school of life—are a rich resource in the church of Crete, for the congregation's edification.

The same is true today. The Lord has placed numerous older women in his churches because he knows we need them. There are so many younger women in the congregation—from mothers of large or small families to sisters with no children or no husband yet. These younger women are, by God's ordinance, helpers to the fathers, office bearers, civil leaders, and businessmen of today and tomorrow. These young women are also mothers to the next generation of church leaders. Obviously these young women play a pivotal role in the life of the church. So they need all the guidance, encouragement and help they can get! By God's ordinance, it is the role of "the older women" to give that help. These older women are under divine obligation to speak with their daughters, daughters-in-law, and other young sisters of congregation.

Certainly, an organized Bible study society is one forum where those conversations can happen. But realistically, it is difficult to open up about life's real burdens to a virtual stranger, let alone in public meetings. Openness requires privacy and intimacy, and that comes with familiarity. Let, then, the older sisters develop the habit of getting into the homes and lives of the younger and engage the challenges younger mothers face as they seek to juggle their responsibilities in marriage, family, and community. What the older have learned over the years in the school of life is meant to be shared with the younger.

Encouragement

The Lord God has granted the Holy Spirit in full measure also to the older sisters. Pentecost is reality: "Even on my male servants and female servants in those days I will pour out my Spirit, and they shall prophesy" (Acts 2:18). In the confidence that the Lord equips to carry out the task assigned, let the older sisters search for innovative ways to touch the younger of the congregation. In this way the senior sisters can "still bear fruit in old age . . . to declare that the Lord is upright; he is my Rock" (Ps 92:14, 15).

Preacher

The God who gave the separate dots in Genesis, Exodus, Leviticus, etc., and caused the Apostle to connect the dots to the inevitable instruction of Titus 2:3 does not change (Num 23:19). That is why every preacher throughout the ages, irrespective of culture or context must "declare these things; exhort and rebuke with all authority." That preacher is to let "no one," not even the older women, "disregard you" (2:15)—for the sound doctrine the preacher must proclaim concerning older women comes from God himself.

POINTS FOR DISCUSSION

1. What is meant by the phrase "older women"? Which age group would you think would be addressed in your congregation with this phrase? What expectations do you have of

these persons in your congregation? Are they being used to the full? If not, how could they be better utilized?

2. The Lord God has assigned to the men the task to give leadership (see previous chapter). Part of giving leadership includes the mandate to teach. So Abraham has to teach his children (Gen 18:19) and the priests (men) are to teach the people of Israel God's ordinances (Lev 10:11). Can you find *commands* in the Scriptures Paul had that women are also to teach? What lesson arises from your findings?

3. For the older women: Paul tells Titus to ensure that the older women in Crete be "reverent in behavior." Are you the sort of older women Paul would want you to be? Perhaps ask the younger women, or the older men, whether your age group comes across as reverent. What could your group do better to be more effective to the younger in your midst?

4. What damage have you experienced in your life as a result of slander? Investigate the Scriptures to find out what the Lord has said about slander. Do you endure slander, or perhaps engage in slander? What can be done to discourage slander in your midst?

5. Why would Paul not want the women of Crete to be addicted to much wine? Is this a problem in your midst? If yes, what can be done about it?

6. How does the gospel of Christ's victory (see Titus 2:11–14) impact on the way older women ought to live and engage the younger?

7. Paul tells Titus that he himself must teach the older men, the older women, the young men and the slaves, while he must rope in the "older women" to teach the young women.

   a. Why is Titus not told to teach the young women himself?

   b. What instruction follows for how this segment of today's church is to receive one-on-one instruction and/or counsel?

c. Are the older women in your church being roped in to train the younger?

8. For the younger women: do you experience a generation gap between yourself and the older women in your midst? In what way is that gap (in part) your fault? What can you do to (help) bridge that gap?

9. If you were the (young) preacher in your congregation (as Titus was on the island), how would you go about "teaching" these older women the "sound doctrine" they need to embrace?

Chapter 7

Young Women

Titus must set in order what remained unfinished in the apostolic labors on the island of Crete. That includes an instruction to "teach what accords with sound doctrine," first to older men, then to older women, and in third place to "young women." Paul's instruction to Titus on the point is this (2:4, 5):

> 1 But as for you, teach what accords with sound doctrine . . . . [Older women . . . are to teach what is good, 4 and so train] the young women to love their husbands and children, 5 to be self-controlled, pure, working at home, kind, and submissive to their own husbands, that the word of God may not be reviled.

Paul's instruction in relation to the young women strikes the modern, Western reader as ridiculously laughable, outdated, even patronizing. Surely, this cannot be God's will for young women—and certainly not in our enlightened day!

Actually, it is God's will, for all generations. Like usual, Paul's instruction did not come out of thin air or from the culture of his day, but was built on God's abiding revelation as first revealed in Paradise, later proclaimed by the patriarchs and prophets, and foreshadowed by the sacrifices and other ceremonies of the law, and finally fulfilled in his only Son. To grasp "what accords with sound doctrine" (Titus 2:1) in relation to young women, we shall need to consider what God had earlier revealed on the matter. We will then look at how Titus must work out this material in Crete, before we draw conclusions for what this means for the church today.

The Foundation in the Old Testament

Genesis 2—Wife

The Lord God put the man he created in the Garden of Eden, with the mandate "to work it and keep it" (Gen 2:15). The Lord observed the man, alone as he was in the Garden, and determined that "it is not good that the man should be alone" (v. 18). On his own the man could not image adequately what God's love, kindness, holiness, and patience, etc., were like, for these qualities come out primarily in *relationships*.[1]

To overcome the lack the Lord observed, he did not set beside Adam a penguin to be his companion, nor did he create a second male as a companion, but he fashioned a new being, a woman (Gen 2:22). Paul in the New Testament explains the significance of this divine act: "woman [was created] for man" (1 Cor 11:9). More, God instituted marriage (Gen 2:24) with the divine intent that the man should be the head and leader, and the woman be "helper" (2:18) to her husband in his God-given task in daily life (2:15). The woman was not created to be a lone-ranger, living for herself independent of man. To the degree that today's way of thinking encourages women to be independent of men (or, for that matter, men to be independent of women), today's thought patterns are simply not biblical.

The fall into sin, of course, complicated greatly the woman's God-assigned task as "helper" to her man. In that fall she had engaged in the serpent's conversation and failed to defer to her husband "who was with her" (Gen 3:6). In his curse upon the woman

---

1. For more detail on this matter, see my book *A Vow to Love*, 67–69.

(Gen 3:16b) God told her she would seek to perpetuate that role reversal throughout the course of history—a reality that would give grief to husband and wife alike all through the ages.

The godly woman, however, regenerated as she is through the renewing work of the Holy Spirit, accepts again the role God assigned in the beginning and so "submits to [her] own husband, as to the Lord"—and therein illustrates how the church is safe with Christ (Eph 5:22–24).

Genesis 1—Mothering

The Lord God created male and female to image what God was like. They were both also to be fruitful and place on our planet more people who could image God (Gen 1:27, 28). The children that would be born to Adam and Eve in Paradise would, however, not know by instinct how to image God; they would need to be taught. In as much as Eve would give birth and nurse the child, she would invariably play a vital role in the child's early formation. Mothering, we realize, is much more than nursing or feeding; mothering is first of all training the child how to live in God's world in a way that images what God is like. Even in Paradise, training was not to start when the child was a toddler or of school age or had become a teenager; had infants been born in Paradise, they would have needed concerted instruction from the day of their birth on how to image God's characteristics of love, joy, peace, patience, kindness, etc. This much is clear then: as Eve busied herself with her tasks beside Adam in the garden, she was at the same time to mold her children, speak to them of their Maker and show them what imaging him looked like in life's changing circumstances. (Fathers, of course, also have a vital role in teaching the children to image God.[2] I am here emphasizing the mother's role because of Titus' emphasis on young women, i.e., mothering.)

---

2. I have written more on this topic in my book *The Privilege of Parenting: A Biblical Explanation of the Form for the Baptism of Infants* (Winnipeg: Premier, 2011) 103–17.

Again, the fall into sin made the task so very much more difficult—if only because both the child and the mother were now inclined to any and every sort of evil (see Gen 6:5; Jer 17:9). Even so, the task of the beginning remained. No mother in God's world was to permit evil, selfish attitudes to grow in the heart of her little one; from the day she gave her child birth in this fallen world, a mother was ever to show what love is, what kindness is, patience is, self-control, etc. In fact, the sinfulness in the child's heart has made the task even more urgent and intense than it would ever have been in Paradise. To say it in Moses' words: "You shall teach [God's words] diligently to your children, and shall talk of them when you sit in your house, and when you walk by the way, and when you lie down, and when you rise. You shall bind them as a sign on your hand" (Deut 6:7,8). Mothering requires full-time commitment.

Proverbs 31—Household

Proverbs 31:10–31 works out in practical terms this instruction from Genesis 1 and 2. The "excellent wife" (31:10) is busy in so many things—buying, selling, importing, helping the poor, etc.; she certainly does not have her hands ever in laundry suds. Yet all she does is driven not by self-fulfillment or a spirit of independence; her agenda instead revolves around her household: "the heart of her husband trusts in her . . . She does him good, and not harm, all the days of her life" (31:11, 12) so that "her husband is known in the gates when he sits among the elders of the land" (31:23). More, she recognizes her role with her children so that "she looks well to the ways of her household . . . Her children rise up and call her blessed; her husband also, and he praises her" (31:27, 28). This woman is not the proverbial "super-mom," but simply a God-fearing woman (31:30b) who takes the principles of Genesis 1 and 2 seriously, and works them out in the economic context of her day.

Application in Crete

The gospel of Jesus Christ had come to Crete, and so Paul saw need with apostolic authority to instruct Titus to set in order the things yet unfinished in the churches of the island (Titus 1:5a). Part of this mandate included the "sound doctrine" Titus had to direct to the "young women" of the congregation. Titus, however, could not easily reach this vital portion of the congregation without endangering his own reputation, and theirs. That is why Paul had Titus instruct the older women (see chapter 5) to train the young women—and that training happens, of course, with the book of Genesis (and the rest of the Bible) laying open on the coffee table: "older women . . . are to teach what is good, and so train the young women to love their husbands and children, to be self-controlled, pure, working at home, kind, and submissive to their own husbands, that the word of God may not be reviled" (Titus 2:3–5).

Loving Their Husband

The first thing Titus must instruct older women to teach the younger is the need to "love their husbands." How striking: Paul's opening instruction is not that the younger wives are to *submit* to their husbands and serve them; it is instead the command to *love* them. The term the Apostle uses has nothing to do with erotic love, but everything to do with the love God displayed in Jesus Christ. The same word appears in John 3:16, "for God so loved the world, that he gave his only Son." The Spirit uses the same word to describe Jesus' work on the cross; Jesus "loved them to the end" (John 13:1), and that is to say that he—who was with the Father in glory from eternity—laid down his life for his own—though he knew that Judas would betray him, Peter would deny him, and all his disciples would desert him in his darkest hour.

The good news of Jesus' self-emptying for sinners had come to Crete and for that reason the believers of Crete were expected to act in a certain manner (Titus 2:11). Specifically, *because* the gospel of Jesus Christ had come to Crete, the pious were to "renounce

ungodliness and worldly passions" (2:12)—which includes denying self in order to love the neighbor as themselves. The closest
neighbor God gave to the "young woman" was obviously her husband, the man with whom she was "one flesh" (Gen 2:24). Younger
women, then, were *duty-bound* to love their husbands as Christ
had loved them; how else could they image what God was like!

So deep was Christ's love that he laid down his life for the
ungodly (Rom 5:8). Paul does not mention whether these young
women's husbands are deserving of love or not, are believers or
not, are decent or not; the young women are simply to do to their
husbands as Christ has done to them. To fail to love in that self-
emptying manner is to send a signal into the community that
prompts the community to speak ill of God's word—and that
would be counterproductive to the advancement of the gospel
(2:5b).

Loving Their Children

The people next closest to the young women are the children the
Lord has entrusted to their care. It is not surprising, then, that
the Apostle next instructs the women to "love their . . . children."
Again, the point is not that these mothers are to be nice to their
children or to feel emotional about them; the point is that they
empty themselves for their children's benefit as Jesus Christ emptied himself for these women. Such self-emptying for the children's
benefit images what the Lord God is like.

The young women of Crete were as affected by the fall into sin
as anyone else. In their midst will have been mothers who would
have preferred to be in the workforce, who felt more fulfilled by
an office job, who loathed housework, or who did not have a "feel"
for children. But Paul's word is categorical; they were to empty
themselves as Christ emptied himself, and so show *love* for their
children. Paul was not so much encouraging particular feelings for
the children as encouraging *actions*; the children should see from
Mom what Jesus' love looked like. That is sound doctrine helpful
for building up the church!

Attitude

The next two terms Paul used to describe what the younger women were to be appear in our translations as "self-controlled" and "pure" (NIV and ESV). The first of these terms appears elsewhere in Scripture to mean "being in one's right mind" (Luke 8:35) or exercising "sober judgment" (Rom 12:3). Right-minded and sober judgment implies that one incorporates all necessary facts in one's decision-making process. That includes the facts mentioned in 2:11: "the grace of God has appeared" in Christ's birth, death and resurrection, "bringing salvation for all people." The young women of the church are to factor that good news into their decisions as they set about loving their husbands and children. Including the gospel in one's decision-making processes is being "right-minded," thinking with "sober judgment."

The term "pure" is used in pagan literature to describe the need to be chaste when you enter the temple of your idol. To the Cretans then—of pagan background as they were—the term echoes the instruction of 2:3, where Paul had told the older women to act in a fashion "befitting a temple" (see chapter 5). The younger women have also received the Holy Spirit (Acts 2:17, 18), and so are temples of the Lord God; they demonstrate that reality by loving their husbands and children as the Lord of the temple loved them.

Working at Home

With the underlying attitudes made clear, the Apostle again comes back to what the teaching of Genesis 1 and 2 requires of New Testament women. He uses a term that translates well as "working at home." The point of the phrase is not that these younger women always have their hands in the sink; that devilish caricature is not at all in agreement with God's intent. The Lord's intent for young women is laid out in Genesis 1 and 2, and drawn out further in passages of Old Testament Scripture as Proverbs 31:10–31. As mentioned above, everything that Mother does (whether at home or at the market or in the office) is geared to what is good for her household, be it first her husband and then her children. That is taking the principles of Genesis 1 and 2 seriously, and working them out in the economic realities of the day. That is "homeworking," where all her activity is directed to what benefits her family. The point is again: the young woman is not to be selfish, but is to serve the family as Christ has served her.

The next term Paul uses, "good," dovetails neatly with the instruction to be "working at home." In her "goodness" (or "kindness," as the term can also be translated), she images God's goodness and kindness to his children in Jesus Christ. So she "looks well to the ways of her household and does not eat the bread of idleness" (Prov 31:27).

Submission

The last instruction the Apostle gives to the young women of the congregation is caught in the phrase "submissive to their own husbands." We realize that here is again a distinct and clear echo of God's instruction in Genesis 2, where God assigned to the man the role of head and to the woman the role of helper. Though the fall into sin has made submission so infinitely more difficult than it was for Eve in Paradise, this posture has remained the will of God despite the fall. On the day of marriage God placed a particular woman beside a particular man, and it is now his will that the woman accept in faith the head God has placed over her and submit to him. After all, "the grace of God has appeared, bringing salvation for all people" (2:11); in life's multiple brokenness there is salvation from the torment of sin through the blood of Jesus Christ. So sinners are made able to "renounce ungodliness and worldly passions" (2:12)—including the desire deep within the woman to resist submission (Gen 3:16b). But the woman who takes the victory of Jesus Christ as real demonstrates her conviction by submitting—in obedience to God's ordinance—to the man

God gave her. She knows the victory of Christ Jesus includes that he poured out his Holy Spirit on the day of Pentecost so that Joel's prophesy was fulfilled: "I will pour out my Spirit on all flesh, and your sons and your daughters shall prophesy" (Acts 2:17). As a temple of the Spirit she has been made able to obey—and knows herself safe in the hands of her faithful God and Savior precisely in the midst of the challenges that come from being subject to a man lacking wisdom or sensitivity. More, in those challenges the older women will keep encouraging the posture of faith: "submissive to their own husbands."[3]

Consequence

As we connect the dots in the material before Titus, we see where the resulting line leads. Modern culture scoffs at the Apostle's instruction to young women because it is so archaic, so demeaning, so sexist to our contemporary sensitivities. We Christians are even inclined to become apologetic about Paul's instruction, and try to explain it away as Paul's (misled) effort that could maybe have worked for the Cretan situation but cannot possibly work in our enlightened day. But the line arising from those connected dots will not justify yielding to that temptation.

Perhaps it is good to note here that the cry for female freedom is not new; cultured folk of Paul's day actually called for the same. Paul, we may be sure, was definitely aware of the thinking of his time, and so was very aware too that his instruction in Titus 2:4–5 was distinctly out of step with the finer tastes of society's movers and shakers. Yet he dared to write what he wrote—and the reason is simply that he unpacked for his day God's unchanging Word as first revealed in Paradise and further unfolded in ensuing generations.

It is also worth noting how the Apostle concludes his instruction concerning the young women. These young women are to behave in the way he describes, he says, "that the word of God

3. For more detail on what submission looks like, the reader is referred to my book *A Vow to Love*, 98–101.

may not be reviled" (2:5b). The statement surprises us. Is it not precisely those instructions of Scripture that have a young woman work at home, submitting to husband, and devoting herself to her children, that make the Word of God look silly? How, then, can Paul say that obedience is necessary lest the Word of God be reviled?

The point here is simply that anyone, whether godly or pagan, who reads the Word of God beginning at Genesis 1 will conclude that the woman was created for the man, that her husband is her head, that she has responsibility for her children, and that her place is in the home. Any honest reader of Scripture, cynical or not, can determine that Paul's instruction in Titus 2:4, 5 is not new material, but simply summarizes what God had earlier revealed. If these Bible readers, then, see Christians ignoring God's instruction in relation to younger women while they claim to treasure the Word of God, then *they* give the unbelieving reader of Scripture reason not to take the rest of God's Word seriously. If one will insist with Titus 2:11 that "the grace of God has appeared, bringing salvation for all people," and if one would encourage those he meets to believe in the good news of Christ crucified for sin, he undermines his own effort when he fails to take Genesis 1 and 2 seriously. If we do not take seriously God's instruction in Genesis 1 and 2 about the place of women, why should we expect another to take seriously other passages of Scripture that describe Christ's death for sin and his resurrection from the dead? If one declines to take Titus 2:4, 5 seriously, on what grounds can he still take Titus 2:11 seriously? The result is simply that the word of God is reviled. If any word of God is to be taken seriously, it must all be taken seriously.

Value

To tie it all up: Paul had left Titus in Crete with the mandate to put in order what was lacking in church life on the island (1:5).

The fact that he in that context included instruction about "young women" can only mean that these sisters have an invaluable role to play in church life.

And this makes good sense. Their husbands, after all, have a leadership role to play in society (Gen 2:15), and to fulfill that task they need a helper (Gen 2:18). As the adage has it: "behind every successful man is a good woman." Similarly, their children are tomorrow's parents and leaders. William Ross Wallace had it right in his memorable poem: "the hand that rocks the cradle is the hand that rules the world."

Young women, then, are not to think of marriage, mothering, and working at home as wasteful or unfulfilling. I do not deny that the task is distinctly a challenge in our fallen world. But the fact that it is a challenge is no reason to flee from the task. Instead, younger women, redeemed as they are in Jesus' blood and renewed by his Spirit, are to lift their eyes above the snotty noses and the piles of laundry, above their tired husband and their own preferences, and fix their attention on what God is doing: he is pleased to use the faithfulness of godly women in their marriages and homes for the well-being of his church. And that the church is run biblically is vital for society's betterment. Not money or business makes the world go round, and not education either; rather, the home is essential for society's welfare. How privileged the position of the godly young woman![4]

Preacher

The God who gave the separate dots in Genesis, Exodus, Leviticus, etc., and caused the Apostle to connect the dots to the inevitable instruction of Titus 2:4, 5 does not change (Num 23:19). That is why every preacher throughout the ages, irrespective of culture or context must "declare these things; exhort and rebuke with all authority." That preacher is to let "no one," not the young women either, "disregard you" (2:15)—for the sound doctrine the preacher

4. See further my book on the form for the baptism of infants, *The Privilege of Parenting*, 119–34.

must proclaim concerning younger women comes from God himself. Since the preacher—male as he is—needs obviously to be sensitive to proper decorum in his interaction with "young women," every preacher does well to insist that the older women keep on teaching this material to the generation following them.

POINTS FOR DISCUSSION

1. Why does Paul not have Titus teach the "young women" himself? What risks would be attached today with "Titus" coming into the homes of young women in your congregation to speak with them about husband and children? What steps are in place in your midst to protect a) your preacher/teacher and b) your young women? Are these steps sufficient?

2. If Paul had sent this letter to your congregation, what age range would you think Paul would want to include with the term "young women"? What sort of questions and issues do the "young women" in your midst struggle with?

3. In searching for answers, young women may turn to reading books, surfing the internet, seeking professional counseling, engaging experienced persons in the community, and staying open with Mom and/or Dad. Evaluate the positives and negatives of each of these options.

4. Do the "young women" in your midst actually treat the "older women" as a valuable resource to turn to for assistance in their struggles? What problems might exist in the minds of the young that prevent them from seeking assistance from the older? What can be done to remove these obstacles?

5. Paul would have the younger women trained to love their husbands and children. Draw out what this "love" for husband and children is to look like. How "out of step" is our society with the biblical norm on this point? How does Paul's instruction match up with the reality in your home? What help (be it practical or educational) do you need so that your

home matches up to Paul's instruction? Where could/would you go to get this help?

6. The Apostle would have the young women "working at home."

   a. Why would he give this instruction?

   b. Is this instruction applicable to our current Western economic realities? Explain your answer.

   c. Is full-time mothering a sufficiently rewarding task in today's world? Why or why not?

   d. How does a mother working outside the home affect the children? Explain why you answer the question as you do.

   e. School, TV, social media, grandmother, and others sometimes play a role in raising one's children. How does the reality in your home conform to God's revealed will?

7. Paul would have the young women be "submissive to their own husbands."

   a. Describe how you feel about that instruction, and explain why you feel as you do.

   b. What could be done to make willing submission easier in your marriage? Remember: the older men and the older women are resources you may tap into for advice and assistance.

   c. What impact does lack of submission have on the generation growing up in your home? Explain your answer.

8. As your neighbors look into your home, is the word of God reviled or honored? Explain why you answer as you do. Perhaps consider what needs to change to have the neighborhood glorify God more on your account.

9. How does the gospel of Christ's victory (see Titus 2:11–14) impact the way young women ought to live?

10. If you were the (young) preacher in your congregation (as Titus was in Crete), how would you go about "teaching" the material of vv. 4 and 5 in your congregation?

Chapter 8

Younger Men

AMONG THE MATTERS THAT needed to be set in order on the island of Crete was also the role God assigned in Scripture to the younger men (2:6–8). Concerning them Paul gave this instruction to Titus:

> 1 But as for you, teach what accords with sound doctrine . . . . 6 Likewise, urge the younger men to be self-controlled. 7 Show yourself in all respects to be a model of good works, and in your teaching show integrity, dignity, 8 and sound speech that cannot be condemned, so that an opponent may be put to shame, having nothing evil to say about us.

As with Paul's instruction concerning older men, older women and young women, we need this time also to turn to the sources from which Paul learned "what accords with sound doctrine" (Titus 2:1), and follow his line of thought. After we have examined the Old Testament Scriptures and the life and teaching of the Savior, we will be in a position to consider more carefully what Paul says about younger men in Crete, and what implications follow for us today.

Who Are the Younger Men?

The phrase "younger men" contrasts with Paul's earlier reference to "older men" (2:2). If the term "older men" describes men who have been around longer than average, the term "younger men" refers to those who have spent less time in the school of life. We tend to put the boundary between these two groups somewhere in the forties or fifties (depending, perhaps, on our own age). We feel more confident to fix the lower limit of the category known as "younger men" somewhere in the twenty to twenty-five year range. Certainly in today's (Western) culture we are not accustomed to talking about too much responsibility for those younger than that.

Adolescents?

Scripture knows two main age brackets in a person's lifetime: childhood and adulthood. In keeping with this distinction of Scripture, Western society (and indeed most societies of the world) long accepted that a person was either a child (with limited expectations and responsibility) or an adult. Two or three generations ago, however, Western culture imported a third grouping between children and adults, namely, adolescents.

An adolescent typically has the strength and energy of an adult, and in many ways the freedoms and opportunities of adults too, but at the same time has the responsibilities of a child. We might say: they are boys who shave. We have come to accept that this is the age when one does dumb things, but we forgive them because, hey, they're still kids-at-heart. There is even a subgroup today known as "kidults"; these are the twenty-somethings who shy away from responsibility and so keep living at home, and have Mom make their lunch and do their laundry while they float from job to job.

This third grouping—let alone the subgroup—is simply not found in Scripture. Rather, Scripture portrays teenagers as responsible before God for their conduct (as is a tween), who need to repent of sin as much as, say, any fifty year old. The Bible simply does not know of a "boy who shaves." In the Bible, if you are no longer a child you are a man, albeit a "young man." (Please do not get impatient; we will get to the scriptural evidence of this statement shortly.) That is the bottom end of the age group Paul addresses in the passage quoted above. He has in mind any male who is no longer a child and not yet an "older man."

Who Is Addressed?

The Lord has preserved this passage of Scripture, of course, not only for the benefit of the "younger men." Older men (Titus 2:2) are to give leadership, and part of the leadership they provide is that they ensure that younger men become what God wants them to be. These older men, then, are meant to learn from Titus 2:6–8 what goals they are to have as they set themselves to mentoring the younger men in the congregation.

Older women (Titus 2:3) are to teach specifically the young women to love their husbands (2:4, 5)—and those husbands are invariably included in the group described as "younger men." As the older women, then, speak to their younger sisters about their (future) husbands, Paul's instruction about younger men will certainly have their interest. The whole congregation, then, can and must learn from God's instruction to the younger men.

The Foundation in the Old Testament

Paradise

Adam was surely no child when God created him, and surely no old man either. In the eye of our minds we see Adam in Paradise as a "younger man" of some twenty, twenty-five, or perhaps thirty years old, in the prime of strength and ability. Notice, then, what responsibilities God expected him to satisfy.

- He was to *image God* (Gen 1:26). Just as the almighty Creator was loving, just, holy, kind, and generous, so Adam was to be loving, just, holy, kind, and generous. Creatures, angels, even God himself should be able to see in the young man Adam something of what God was like.

- In second place, he was to *rule over* all creation (Gen 1:26). This young man received a kingly function, with all creatures under his dominion. Notice: God did not let Adam hang around for several years until he was older and/or made wise through years of experience before all creation was placed under his feet. As soon as he was created, God gave him the mandate to "work" the garden and "keep" it (Gen 2:15). The term "keep" describes the task of protecting the garden from enemies—and God knew full well that a creature as cunning as Satan would attack the garden through his insidious temptation. Yet God entrusted the garden to the care of this young man.

- Further, the young man Adam was told to be *fruitful* (Gen 1:28). We realize that the command to be fruitful does not refer simply to having children, but includes the responsibility of raising the children so that the next generation would learn how to image God and be effective rulers of God's world too.

- God said too that it was not good for the man to be alone, and so God created a woman to be "helper" to the man (Gen 2:18). The man in turn was to accept the helper God gave him, and give her leadership and protection.

God's instructions to Adam, then, point up that Adam was expected to *embrace responsibility*. Young men of subsequent generations were, obviously, to do the same. The biblical picture of (young) manhood is not one of loafing or playing games or just letting things happen. Rather, a biblically faithful man welcomes responsibility and takes initiative. This is the "sound doctrine" Titus is to teach the younger men of Crete, and it is equally the "sound doctrine" the older men are to impress on the younger, and what older women are to teach the younger to expect of their husbands.

Fall

The fall into sin made carrying out this glorious responsibility impossibly difficult. Work became a slog and a burden (Gen 3:19). Weeds appeared not just in gardens and fields (Gen 3:18), but also in one's character and in interpersonal relations. Tensions characterized marriage (Gen 3:16b), and children would reduce a man to tears (Gen 4:8). We understand clearly why the Preacher describes all as vanity, a burden, a groan (Eccl 1:2). "What has a man from all his toil and striving of heart with which he toils beneath the sun?" (Eccl 2:22). The creature fashioned to image God, rule over God's world, and raise more image-bearers—what glorious privilege!—encounters so much frustration.

Understood

Despite the destructive effects of the fall into sin, several figures of the Old Testament demonstrate that they fully understood God's intent for young men. Consider the following:

- Joseph was seventeen years old when his father sent him to check up on how his brothers were faring as they tended the family flocks (Gen 37:2). He was also, then, seventeen years old when he was sold as a slave to Egypt. As a young man he ended up in Potiphar's house. Yet he readily embraced responsibility, so that his master "put him in charge of all that he had" (Gen 39:4). Not too many years later, perhaps in his early twenties, Joseph was imprisoned "where the king's prisoners were confined (39:20), yet took the initiative to embrace whatever responsibility rolled his way—and so "the keeper of the prison put Joseph in charge of all the prisoners" (39:22). He took control of his feelings so that he did not waste his energy with being angry at his brothers or full of pity for himself. When his family came to Egypt twenty years after he was sold, he was still a relatively "young man" of thirty-seven—but ruler over the entire country.

- David was a teenager when he was entrusted with his father's sheep. As a teenager he fought off a lion and a bear, and was called to play the lyre to King Saul. As a "youth" he volunteered to fight Goliath (1 Sam 17:42). In his twenties he led Israel out to battle as Saul's commander, then fled from Saul and, though persecuted, refused to kill him. Young though he was, he understood what manhood was about; he embraced responsibility and so made hard decisions. By the time he was thirty, he was king over God's people Israel.

- Daniel was a young man, likely yet a teenager, when he was taken as prisoner to Babylon. As young as he was, he took a stand against the unclean food the palace prescribed (Dan 1:8). Again, in his youth he used the opportunities he received to learn what he could. So, when God elevated him as a young man to a position of power and leadership in a foreign land, he was ready for the challenge.

These three young men acted in line with God's expectation for men as revealed in Paradise. They understood that youth was not a time for mooching, nor a time to live off others; being young men meant that they were to embrace responsibility to image God and rule over what was entrusted to them—especially them*selves*.

Jesus

The ultimate biblical example of what a "young man" was to look like is none else than Jesus of Nazareth. He was "like his brothers in every respect" (Heb 2:17), and that includes the reluctance some have to embrace responsibility. But the Scripture says of this young man that though he was tempted in every respect as we are, he never gave himself to sin (Heb 4:15). In his teenage years, and in his twenties too, he made it his business to image God in all he did, and made it his business too to rule over whatever God entrusted to his care—including first of all *himself*, be that in guarding his mouth or restraining his hormones or willingly taking initiatives.

At thirty years of age—truly a young man still!—he took up his public ministry in Israel, preaching the good news of the kingdom of God in the face of stiff opposition, healing the sick and raising the dead. In the process he denied himself for the benefit of those the Father entrusted to him, even embracing the cursed cross and the heavy judgment of God for the benefit of the undeserving. Herein he demonstrated precisely what God intended for all men back in Paradise already; they are to embrace responsibility, and so take initiative to advance the kingdom of God. In fact, Jesus' embrace of the responsibility that belongs to being a man brought about that "the grace of God has appeared, bringing salvation for all people" (Titus 2:11). Paul drew out the same lesson elsewhere: "Husbands, love your wives, as Christ loved the church and gave himself up for her, that he might sanctify her . . . In the same way husbands should love their wives as their own bodies" (Eph 5:25–28). Jesus carried out perfectly what God intended for younger men in Paradise, and so is *the* example all younger men are to follow.

Paul Unpacks

The Apostle Paul wants to build up church life in Crete. He learned from God's Old Testament instruction and saw fulfilled in Jesus' example what the Lord God wanted of younger men on the island of Crete. Titus, now, must "teach what accords with sound doctrine," and in relation to younger men that means that Titus must insist that they "be self-controlled" (as our translation has it).

Sober-Minded

The term Paul uses to describe what younger men are to be is difficult to translate. The NIV and the ESV render it with the term "self-controlled"; the NKJV has "sober-minded"; the NASB has "sensible." The same term appears in Mark 5:15 in relation to the demoniac after the pigs drowned in the sea; the locals found the man "in his right mind." In Romans 12:3 Paul uses this same term to instruct his readers "not to think of himself more highly than he ought to think, but to think with *sober judgment.*"

The point is this. God created us to "rule over" all creatures, including ourselves. With the fall into sin, we became slaves to sin so that Satan ruled over us. Christ, however, perfect (younger) man that he was, conquered sin and Satan and so brought salvation for all people (Titus 2:11). Sin, then, is no longer our master, no more than the exorcised demons were now master of the demoniac of Mark 5. Instead, Christ has poured out his Spirit so that we can again be the *men* God wants us to be.

Men are meant to embrace responsibility. Paul, now, would have Titus urge younger men to take seriously the victory of Jesus Christ as they make decisions day by day about what to do. They are, in other words, to think of themselves with the "sober judgment" that comes with believing the gospel of Calvary: since you are no longer slaves to sin—that is reality—but are once again God's possession through Jesus Christ—that is reality, too!—you do not *have* to give in to sin and temptation, you *can* resist the evil one. Factoring that victory into one's decision-making process is being *sober-minded*, and yes, it leads to a life of *self-control*.

Verse 12

Verse 12 logically follows, and works out what this level-headedness looks like in the midst of life's temptations. Christ's victory "train[s] us to renounce ungodliness and worldly passions, and to live self-controlled, upright, and godly lives in the present age." And yes, the word translated as self-controlled in 2:12 is the same critical word as the Apostle used in 2:6 about the younger men needing to be "self-controlled," "sober-minded," level-headed, and realistic because of Calvary. Christ has broken Satan's back; let "younger men" factor that reality into their decision-making processes. That is taking responsibility properly.

I do need to add: "the present age" is *not* a reference to the younger years where one might think it okay to give in to sinful urges, and just live it up; this "present age" is instead the period between Christ's victory on the cross and his return in glory (see 2:13). His victory on the cross guarantees the final great act of history, the day when he comes to judge the living and the dead. That reality again prompts the "young man" to a particular level-headedness as he factors this forthcoming return into the decisions he makes—whether to buy that car, pursue that career opportunity, invest in his family, plan his vacation, etc.

Titus

This sort of lifestyle represented a huge challenge for the younger men in Crete. Paul had earlier caught the feel of the island's culture in the proverb he had quoted with agreement: "Cretans are always liars, evil beasts, lazy gluttons" (1:12). It is a mindset that encourages folk to do whatever they feel like doing—and young men (that includes teenagers) are certainly inclined to do precisely that. With the Christian faith new to the island, the Christian "younger men" had few role models to look up to.

That is why Paul told Titus that he needed to be a good example for these young men. Said the Apostle to Titus: "show yourself in all respects to be a model of good works, and in your teaching show integrity, dignity, and sound speech that cannot be condemned" (2:7). Titus, the Apostle's "true child in a common faith" (1:4), had learned how to live the Christian life from the Apostle himself, and had learned from him how to model that lifestyle also. As preacher on the island, and a young man at that, Titus needed to be aware that other young Christian men in Crete would be watching how he lived out the gospel of Christ's victory in his daily responsibilities. How he factored Christ's triumph into his daily decisions needed to demonstrate that he renounced ungodliness and worldly passions (2:12), and instead gave himself to good works. More, his teaching could not have the empty ring of liars' big talk (1:10), but needed to display integrity, dignity, and soundness (2:7, 8).

Here is a reality true for every preacher/teacher of all times, indeed true for all office bearers and leaders. Anyone entrusted with the task of preaching and teaching the gospel of Christ's victory needs be aware of his role as a model of Christian living. Brothers, we are created and recreated to image God, and so to have dominion over whatever God has entrusted to our care in the same way as the Lord exercises dominion. Christ Jesus emptied himself for the sake of his bride, the church. As teachers and preachers of this good news, we must—if we wish the gospel to be credible—follow this example in all our conduct and our words. The young men of the congregation need us!

Conclusion

What, then, is the vital role Paul sees for younger men in contributing to healthy church life, be it long ago on the island of Crete or today in the twenty-first century? Younger men are to take seriously whatever responsibility God gives them (whether it is over their time, energy, schooling, a vehicle, a house, a wife, children, themselves, work, etc.) and *consistently factor in the victory of Jesus Christ over sin* as they make decisions pertaining to the responsibilities God has given. Then there is no place for ungodliness, and plenty of space for godly lives. Such a lifestyle advertises the church wonderfully.

In the churches today we see, by God's grace, many younger men, from teens to forties, making responsible decisions, and so contributing positively to church life. I refer to young men genuinely professing the faith at school and in recreation, at work and in the community. We see young men presenting their children for baptism and taking seriously the vow involved with that. We see young men devoted to their wives and families, and stretching themselves for service in God's kingdom. It is reason for gratitude.

We also see young men who do not stretch themselves as much as possible for the greater glory of the Lord God. We see some young men content with a basic job; they come home from work to chill in front of the TV or spend the evening on the internet, and others who pour themselves into sport. There is nothing wrong with sport, nor with relaxing in front of the TV, or even doing simply a hands-on job. But there is a problem if one spends no time or energy to grow oneself for increased responsibility tomorrow. It is for responsibility that God created men, and so men *must* read, study, and prepare for leadership roles in the future.

Manhood is not to be measured by how much hair you can grow, or how big a truck you can drive, or how much beer you can drink, or how good you are on your skates, or how big a fish you can catch. Without knocking any of these things, none of them catches what God created *men* to do.

What God wants of *men* is that we *embrace responsibility*, to the point that we work with Christ's victory in every decision we make—every moment of every day, or night. What does that look like? It *follows the example of Jesus Christ* in his self-emptying for his bride. He is *the younger man* who took responsibility for those God entrusted to his care, namely, the people God gave him, and so laid down his life for his own. That is the sensible, sober-minded, level-headed example the Lord has given younger men to follow.

Preacher

The God who gave the separate dots in Genesis, Exodus, Leviticus, etc., and caused the Apostle to connect the dots to the inevitable instruction of Titus 2:6–8 does not change (Num 23:19). That is why every preacher throughout the ages, irrespective of culture or context must "declare these things; exhort and rebuke with all authority." That preacher is to let "no one," not even (fellow) youth, "disregard you" (2:15)—for the sound doctrine the preacher must proclaim concerning younger men comes from God himself.

POINTS FOR DISCUSSION

1. If Paul had sent this letter to your congregation, what age bracket in your congregation would you think Paul would

want to include with the term "younger men"? What sort of questions and issues do the "younger men" in your midst struggle with?

2. It is not unheard of for young men to try to be self-sufficient, and so seek answers within themselves. Would you condone this? Why or why not? Evaluate the positives and negatives of other options young men may turn to (including: reading books, surfing the internet, seeking professional counseling, engaging experienced persons in the community, and staying open with Mom and/or Dad) and then rank them in order of actual benefit.

3. Do the "younger men" in your midst actually treat the "older men" as a valuable resource to turn to for assistance in their struggles? What problems might exist in the minds of the young that prevent them from seeking assistance from the older?

4. Discuss the level of responsibility Adam had immediately after his creation. Are you comfortable in seeing today's young men have that same level of responsibility? Why or why not? Familiarize yourself with Samuel's temptations and challenges as described in 1 Samuel 1–4. How old do you picture him to have been? How did he handle responsibility?

5. Paul would have the younger men exercise *sober judgment*. What would obedience to that term look like? What does this imply for a youth's commitment to Jesus Christ?

6. How does the gospel of Christ's victory (see Titus 2:11–14) impact the way younger men ought to live?

7. Paul had indicated that young women were to be "submissive to their own husbands." How are the young men in your midst making it pleasant for their wives to submit to them? Does more need to be done to ensure the young women feel safe with their men?

8. As your neighbors look into your life as a young man, do they have reason to speak evil of you or not? Explain why you

answer as you do. Perhaps consider what needs to change to have the neighborhood glorify God more on your account.

9. For the older: Titus, in his role of leadership on the island, is to be a model for the younger men around him. How are your (church) leaders good role models for the younger men in your midst? What can you do to help the leaders be better role models?

10. For the younger: today's younger men are tomorrow's older men, folk from whom leadership is expected. What are you doing to prepare yourselves for tomorrow's task as leaders in marriage and family, church, business, and community in general? What more could be done?

11. If you were the (young) preacher in your congregation (as Titus was on the island), how would you go about "teaching" these younger men the "sound doctrine" they need to embrace?

Chapter 9

Slaves

THE LAST OF THE groupings within the congregation the Apostle instructs Titus to address are the slaves (2:1, 9-10):

> 1 But as for you, teach what accords with sound doctrine . . . 9 Slaves are to be submissive to their own masters in everything; they are to be well-pleasing, not argumentative, 10 not pilfering, but showing all good faith, so that in everything they may adorn the doctrine of God our Savior.

The term "slave" sends our thoughts instantly to those dark pages of history where people bought and sold other people as if they were cattle. Such conduct, irrespective of who did it, was and remains reprehensible, and a great evil before God. To the degree that buying and selling people as chattel in a market is not part of our contemporary culture, we feel that this passage has little to say to us. But that thought is wrong. What the Apostle says here about the slaves of Crete teaches us much about how employees today have opportunity to illustrate the gospel in how they do their work. In that role they have great impact on what the community ends up thinking about the gospel—and so to contributing to the Lord's church gathering work.

What Paul tells Titus to teach slaves is again "what accords with sound doctrine" (2:1), and so drawn from God's earlier revelation. As with Paul's instruction in relation to older men and women, and younger women and men, we shall need to consider first what Paul learned from God's earlier revelation on the subject before we come to Paul's specific instructions about the conduct of the slaves of Crete and what consequences follow for ourselves. First, though, we need to set the stage with a couple of introductory thoughts.

Place of a Slave

Economic System

A concordance illustrates that the Bible mentions slavery often, both in the Old Testament as well as in the New Testament. This does not mean, however, that the Lord God approves of slavery. Rather, the Lord took seriously the economic cultures in which his people lived (and every culture is obviously affected by sin), and showed his people how they were to live within their imperfect culture. The point is not whether slavery, or capitalism or communism for that matter, is right or wrong, but rather the *attitude* God's people portray as they live within the economic system of their environment. In Titus 2:9, 10, the Lord through Paul instructed his people in Crete how they were to act within their context of slavery. That is why employees and employers in any economic system can learn from Paul's instruction to Titus.

Roman Context

Family life in Paul's day was structured differently than family life is structured in our day. There were, for example, no old-age homes or fully serviced gated communities for seniors; in Roman culture grandparents, parents, and children lived together in one home as a close-knit family unit. If by God's grace the head of the family came to faith, the whole household was baptized and so became Christian (as the examples of Lydia and the Philippian jailer demonstrate, Acts 16:15, 33–34).[1]

Slaves were part of the family. The family had possibly bought this slave at the market or had received this slave as booty from a war, or perhaps the slave in question was born of slaves in the family. These slaves did the laborious work in the family, and so contributed greatly to the economy. For some slaves, life was hard inasmuch as a cruel master had the legal right to whip his slave for any infraction, could sell a slave, and even have him killed. For those who had a good master, slavery gave security because the master provided housing, food, and other necessities. In the latter case, there was much in common with today's employees; good employers look well after those they employ.

Titus was to complete what was yet unfinished in Crete. So he had to teach the congregations, including the slaves, all that God had revealed—and that included specific instruction about their role as slaves. Though slaves were commonly seen as forming the bottom rung on the social ladder, the Apostle understood that the Lord entrusted to them a vital role in the growth of the gospel on the island. Before we draw out in more detail what that means for ourselves today, we need to turn to what God had revealed in the past. How was Paul's instruction to Titus formed by God's earlier revelation?

Old Testament Foundation

The term "slave" appears frequently in the Old Testament. Sometimes the term describes very subhuman practices wherein people were treated as cattle. Ishmaelite slave traders, for example, sold Joseph to the highest bidder in Egypt (Gen 39:1). The people of Israel were subjected to such cruel slavery in Egypt that they cried out in despair (Exod 2:23). Other times the term is used to describe what happened in Israel when a fellow Israelite became so indebted that he had to sell himself to pay his debt (Lev 25:39).

1. Elsewhere I have written extensively on why the entire household was baptized. See *The Privilege of Parenting*, 63–74.

In relation to the latter case, the Lord God gave specific laws to regulate how slaves were to be treated.

Israelite Law

The Lord insisted that his people treat their slaves with respect. For example, "if your brother, a Hebrew man or a Hebrew woman, is sold to you, he shall serve you six years, and in the seventh year you shall let him go free from you. And when you let him go free from you, you shall not let him go empty-handed. You shall furnish him liberally out of your flock, out of your threshing floor, and out of your winepress. As the Lord your God has blessed you, you shall give to him" (Deut 15:12–14). In fact, the care the Israelite was to give to his Hebrew slave was to reflect the redemption they received from God: "You shall remember that you were a slave in the land of Egypt, and the Lord your God redeemed you; therefore I command you this today" (Deut 15:15). So good was the care to be that God sanctioned the decision of the slave who decided not to use the opportunity to regain his freedom in the seventh year but preferred to stay with his master (Deut 15:16–17). If on the other hand a Hebrew slave ran away from his master (a likely sign of mistreatment), God commanded the neighbor to whom he fled not to return him to his master but to give him asylum (Deut 23:15–16). This material makes it plain that slavery in Israel had much more in common with the place of today's employees than with the slave trade so cruelly attested through history.

Under God

Yet to understand Paul well we need to reach beyond the Mosaic Law to God's revelation in Genesis 1. That chapter of Scripture presents us with the almighty Creator who spoke his sovereign word, and as a result the earth became an orderly and organized home for the human race. As climax of his creating work, the Lord God fashioned man with the privileged position of imaging what

God was like—including that he should "have dominion over" all God had created (Gen 1:26–28). As David put it: "Thou hast made him a little lower than God" (Ps 8:5, NASB).[2] On a scale of one to ten, with God himself at ten, he placed man at nine! What lofty privilege! Yet his place is *under* God, as his servant, his slave. (Note: in the Bible the words "servant" and "slave" translate the same Hebrew word, and—despite the differences we hear in those terms in English—mean the same thing.) People are not free agents permitted to think or act independently of their Maker; in their place under God people are (meant to be) "slaves of God" (Rom 6:22). This principle is basic to the structure of God's creation ordinance. When Paul describes himself to Titus as "a servant/slave of God" (1:1), he ultimately says nothing new; every person is created to be a servant/slave of God—be it that we (like Joseph in Potiphar's house) are "in charge of all" God's house (see Gen 39:4).

The Fall

In Adam and Eve the human race rebelled against God (Gen 3:6) and so rejected his lofty place as a nine-under-God. Instead of being a "slave to God" people became "slaves of sin" (Rom 6:17, 20). Directly after the fall, the Lord God described what life in a fallen world would look like. He spoke of curse and weeds, of thorns and thistles, of pain and sickness and death (Gen 3:16–19). The frustration he spoke about did not describe only the physical weeds and sicknesses, but also the relational ones where interactions between people in the workforce get twisted, selfish, and even so oppressive that the one enslaves the other to do his will. Israel experienced such oppression so bitterly in the days of their bondage to the Egyptians. In varying degrees the same sort of thing can (and does) happen in any economic system man has since thought up. One human enslaving another is a bitter fruit of the fall into sin, and certainly not what God intended when he created the human race. Being enslaved is a far, far cry from being a nine-under-God!

2. This, in fact, is the literal—and accurate—translation of the Hebrew.

Deliverance

By the grace of God deliverance from slavery to sin has come through the work of Jesus Christ. As Paul writes to Titus: "For the salvation of God has appeared, bringing salvation for all people" through "Jesus Christ, who gave himself for us to redeem us from all lawlessness" (2:11, 14). The salvation Christ obtained does not set us free from the lordship of sin and Satan so that now we can be our own boss; rather, his redemption restores us to God to be "his own possession" (2:14)—as we were in Paradise. As Paul puts it elsewhere: "you who were once slaves of sin have . . . become slaves of righteousness" (Rom 6:17, 18). This is the redemption prefigured in Israel's release from Egypt, as God himself put it when he gave his people his law at Mt Sinai: "I am the Lord your God, who brought you out of the land of Egypt, out of the house of slavery" (Exod 20:2).

Implications in Crete

Paul the "servant of God" (Titus 1:1) must ensure that the Christians of Crete hear the whole counsel of God, and so instructs Titus to complete what was unfinished. Part of God's instruction addresses the slaves on the island. These slaves have been redeemed through Jesus' blood to be God's "own possession" (2:14), and so—says Paul—Titus must teach slaves "to be submissive to their own masters in everything; they are to be well-pleasing, not argumentative, not pilfering, but showing all good faith, so that in everything they may adorn the doctrine of God our Savior" (2:9, 10).

Be Submissive

The term rendered for us as "be submissive . . . in everything" is put together in the Greek in such a way as to convey the notion that slaves need to make a point of *submitting themselves* to their masters. In other words, their submission is to be voluntary, a willing act on the slaves' part and not the result of coercion. Notice that Paul does not distinguish between whether the master is Christian or not, cruel or considerate. Either way, the Christian slave is to *submit himself.*

The point is striking. Are slaves not simply to do what their masters tell them to do, without thinking? But here Paul wants Titus to tell slaves in Crete to *make a decision*, one that acknowledges obedience to a higher authority than their human masters. The reason is not hard to understand. Every person was created to be a nine-under-God, and so responsible to obey God as well as responsible to have dominion over whatever parts of God's creation God has entrusted to that person. The fall into sin and its consequences did not change that blessed reality, so that at a minimum one's mind, and indeed one's self, remains your personal responsibility.

Every Christian is a slave of the Master, God Almighty. It has pleased this Master to assign to each of his slaves a certain place and task in life—to some specifically as slave to a particular human master. The Christian slave is to accept that reality, and so work where the Master has placed him (see 1 Cor 7:20–24). More, this God has sent his Son to pay for sin (Titus 2:11) so that the identity of the Christian slave is determined ultimately not by his slavery but by his adoption into God's family as his much loved child. In the house of this Father there is no place for "ungodliness and worldly passions" (2:12). Instead, as the child of God waits for Christ's appearing (2:13), there is place only for good works (2:14b). That includes that one accept what the divine Master has given, and so serving him in the place and task assigned—even if that includes being a slave to an earthly master. That is the attitude required in Titus 2:9a: "slaves are to be submissive to their own masters in everything."

Be Well-Pleasing

The service the Lord requires from these slaves is also to "be well-pleasing." Note that Paul does not say that slaves must "try to please,"[3] but must *succeed* in pleasing their masters: "be well-pleasing." It is striking that the term Paul uses appears numerous other times in Scripture,[4] but always in relation to pleasing God. This verse would appear to be the only exception, with human masters now being the judges of the slaves' effort. But given that elsewhere God is always the judge, and given too how fickle human masters can be, surely the point is not so much that the earthly master is to be well-pleased with your service, but the divine Master first of all. As one serves this divine Master well, the earthly master also receives good reason to be pleased.

To color in what the behavior of the "well-pleasing" slave looks like, the Apostle lists a number of characteristics.

Not Argumentative

The Christian slave does not mouth off to his master, does not quarrel with him. This instruction, of course, addresses the Cretan habit of big mouthing one another. Paul had agreed with the Cretan prophet who had said, "Cretans are always liars, evil beasts, lazy gluttons" (1:12), and in step with that sad reality had mentioned that in Crete "there are many who are insubordinate, empty talkers and deceivers" (1:10). Later in his letter he will instruct Titus to "avoid foolish controversies . . . dissensions, and quarrels about the law" (3:9). The point is that Cretan slaves lived in a culture that embraced confrontational and belligerent behavior, and so were tempted to be the same. But the Christian slave has been renewed by the Holy Spirit, and so brings forth the fruit of the Spirit: love, peace, kindness, gentleness, self-control (Gal 5:22, 23). Any response the Christian slave would give to his master must, then, be couched in respective submission and seek his master's benefit.

---

3. As the NIV erroneously renders the text.

4. Rom 12:1, 2; 14:18; 2 Cor 5:9; Eph 5:10; Phil 4:18; Col 3:20; Heb 13:21.

Not Pilfering

The slave is not to "pilfer" or steal from his master. The fact of the matter is that the Lord God owns all things (Ps 24:1), and has entrusted specific items of his creation to the care of particular individuals. Relative to his master, the slave has received little in terms of material possessions. He is, then, so obviously dependent on his God—and God supplies his needs through the master God set over him. It is an expression of his faith that the slave entrust himself to the care of his God, and so resist the temptation to say that the master owes him this or that, or is negligent in looking after him, and concluding that he is justified in helping himself to his master's possessions. To do so would be to pilfer. Again, in the context of Cretan culture—"Cretans are always liars, evil beasts, lazy gluttons"—Christian slaves who made a point of not stealing undoubtedly stood out as distinctly different.

Show Good Faith

In contrast to the argumentative spirit and the pilfering Paul has condemned, he insists that the Christian slave is to "show all good faith." The emphasis lies on the word "good" so that the point of the instruction is that the master is made to see the goodness and wholesomeness of what it means to trust in the greater Master Jesus Christ "who gave himself for us to redeem us" (2:14). On account of Jesus' work, then, the Christian slave can—and must—give his all to serving the human master Christ has set over him. This attitude contrasts starkly with fallen human nature, as Paul admits in Titus 3:3: "For we ourselves were once foolish, disobedient, led astray, slaves to various passions and pleasures, passing our days in malice and envy, hated by others and hating one another." But by God's grace this has changed in the hearts of the slaves Paul wants Titus to address, for "when the goodness and loving kindness of God our Savior appeared, he saved us . . . according to his own mercy, by the washing of regeneration and renewal of the Holy Spirit . . . so that . . . we might become heirs according to the hope of eternal life" (Titus 3:4, 5, 7). Therefore the fruit of the Spirit (Gal 5:22–23) determines how you carry out your God-assigned role as slave.

In Short

Being content with the place one's divine Master has assigned is, we realize, an attitude all God's people need to embrace, irrespective of the economic culture in which one may live. Whether one was a slave in ancient Crete or is an employee in a state-of-the-art office in downtown Toronto or is a laborer in a third world factory makes ultimately no difference; our divine Master in Jesus Christ has given us a particular place with a specific boss, where our time and energy and expertise is "sold" to him in return for a payout of some form. As we do our task in submission to the person God sets over us in our work, it will not do to reflect attitudes of selfishness and entitlement so prevalent in our fallen society, but it is fitting—trusting in God as we do—to submit to the boss, not talking back, not stealing, showing that we are trustworthy, and in it all being well-pleasing to God and man alike. In a word, we are to serve *as Christ served us*.

Purpose

Why, now, did Paul mention slaves in his letter to Titus? His intent in the letter, we recall, was to ensure that the unfinished be completed, and that included that Titus had to teach sound doctrine so that God's revealed will would be brought to bear on the lives of the new believers on the island so that in turn church life would flourish in Crete. Do folk so underprivileged as slaves have a role to play in the health of the church? Paul's answer is Yes, and he explains why he includes slaves in the list of those whom Titus must teach: "so that in everything they may adorn the doctrine of God our Savior" (2:10).

Adorn

The term translated as 'adorn' was commonly used to describe a monument one might set up in order to draw attention to some famous person—be it a favored citizen of a community, or even oneself. Slaves were in no (financial) position to set up such a shrine. Yet Paul says that slaves under God are in fact so rich in Jesus Christ that they *are* able to set up a memorial for "the doctrine of God our Savior." How, we wonder, can they make the doctrine of God famous? That, of course, is by adopting the lifestyle Paul had just described. Through their willing submission to the master God set over them, and their being "well-pleasing, not argumentative, not pilfering, but showing all good faith," these slaves would become living advertisements and monuments of the triumph (2:11–12) of Jesus Christ. Such conduct contrasts with what is typical in society, and so serves to build up the church in Crete. The church of Jesus Christ, then, is built up not just on Sunday or when elders make their visits, but is built up any day of the week in the factory, the gravel pit, the construction site—wherever masters might send their slaves to work. This is "lifestyle evangelism"!

Evangelism

We appreciate the consequence of what the Apostle says. Many of us have received from God our Master a place under a boss or employer, so that we spend our energies in an office, on a factory floor, at a construction site, in somebody's garden, driving someone's truck, laboring in a classroom, etc. The instruction of the Apostle is that the victorious Christ is using each of us in his church-building work through the manner in which we carry out our daily tasks. Paul considers that manner essential; our attitude in our work either promotes the gospel or maligns the Word of God, be it to the boss or to fellow employees or to the public who sees how we work. What we do anywhere in public life always touches on *church building*!

Preacher

The God who gave the separate dots in Genesis, Exodus, Leviticus, etc., and caused the Apostle to connect the dots to the inevitable instruction of Titus 2:9, 10 does not change (Num 23:19). That is why every preacher throughout the ages, irrespective of culture or context must "declare these things; exhort and rebuke with all authority." That preacher is to let "no one," not even a slave, "disregard you" (2:15)—for the sound doctrine the preacher must proclaim concerning slaves comes from God himself.

Points for Discussion

1. What is meant by the term "slaves"? What role did slaves play in Cretan economy and in the home where they labored? How does that compare to the role of today's employee? What are the questions and issues employees struggle with today?

2. What Old Testament instruction bears upon Paul's words to Titus about what he is to teach slaves? How does that instruction speak to today's employees? How can today's employees work with David's description of the lofty position God has given to mankind as little lower than God (see Ps 8:5)?

3. How does the gospel of Christ's victory (see Titus 2:11–14) impact the way slaves ought to live?

4. What sort of guidance and encouragement could older men or women give the slaves of Titus' day? How can retirees in your midst offer encouragement and assistance to employees today? How can the connections between the retired and the employed in your midst be improved?

5. Discuss the actual impact employees in your midst have in terms of how the gospel is seen in your community. Do your employees in fact "adorn the gospel of God our Savior"? What could be done to improve public assessment of the gospel?

6. Paul does not instruct Titus in relation to slave owners. Even so, how would Jesus' victory as described in Titus 2:11–14 impact on how today's employers treat their employees?

7. If you were the (young) preacher in your congregation (as Titus was on the island), how would you go about "teaching" these employees the "sound doctrine" they need to embrace?

Chapter 10

Cross-Centered Motive

PAUL HAD PLUNDERED GOD'S earlier revelation for instruction as he considered what needed to be done to complete the work of the gospel begun on the island of Crete. Yet the power driving Paul's conclusions was not simply that God had said this or that in bygone generations (authoritative as that is). Rather, what gave force and strength to the conclusions Paul gleaned from the Old Testament was what had recently happened in Jesus Christ. In Titus 2:11–15 Paul put it like this:

> 11 For the grace of God has appeared, bringing salvation for all people, 12 training us to renounce ungodliness and worldly passions, and to live self-controlled, upright, and godly lives in the present age, 13 waiting for our blessed hope, the appearing of the glory of our great God and Savior Jesus Christ, 14 who gave himself for us to redeem us from all lawlessness and to purify for himself a people for his own possession who are zealous for good works.
>
> 15 Declare these things; exhort and rebuke with all authority. Let no one disregard you.

Space for Grace

Titus surely understood well what Paul meant with the phrase "the grace of God has appeared, bringing salvation." As Paul's "true child in a common faith" (1:4), Titus understood Paul's way of thinking and of expressing himself—a manner informed by the Old Testament.

Ever since the fall into sin in Paradise, the human race was deserving of God's judgment (Gen 2:17). God, however, deferred the judgment so as to give opportunity for grace to do its work; God gave space for the offspring of the woman to be born and triumph over the offspring of the serpent (Gen 3:15). Time and again God had this victory foreshadowed through the shedding of an animal's blood in place of the sinner's; an animal died instead of Adam and Eve (Gen 3:21), Noah (Gen 8:20,21), Isaac (Gen 22:13), and countless others. The people of Israel in Egypt were no better than the Egyptians, yet were spared the death of their firstborn because a lamb died in their place (Exod 12:13). At Mt. Sinai the Lord gave instructions about the sacrifices his sinful people had to make daily in the tabernacle; repeatedly a lamb had to die in place of the sinner (Lev 1–5).

One New Testament writer summed up this Old Testament instruction with these words: "under the law almost everything is purified with blood, and without the shedding of blood there is no forgiveness of sins" (Heb 9:22). This is why Jesus Christ had to come; "he has appeared once for all at the end of the ages to put away sin by the sacrifice of himself" (Heb 9:26). As "the Lamb of God who takes away the sin of the world" (John 1:29), Jesus did not avoid the agony of the cross, but obediently laid down his life as a ransom for many (Mark 10:45). This is the gospel Paul proclaimed to Jews and Gentiles alike as he had opportunity: "Let it be known to you therefore, brothers, that through this man forgiveness of sins is proclaimed to you, and by him everyone who believes is freed from everything from which you could not be freed by the law of Moses" (Acts 13:38–39).

That is the gospel Paul now describes to Titus with those wonderful words: "the grace of God has appeared." The abundant mercy of God proclaimed in the Old Testament, whereby sinners would not suffer the penalty their transgressions deserve but receive instead forgiveness and even adoption as sons of God, has now "appeared." The Son of God was born in Bethlehem (Christmas), then went to the cross to atone for sin (Good Friday), and triumphed (Easter)! He "gave himself for us to redeem us from all lawlessness" (Titus 2:14). No longer are sinners slaves to sin and so committed to lawlessness, but they are forgiven of sin and made heirs of "eternal life"—even as "God, who never lies, promised before the ages began" (Titus 1:2). "The grace of God has appeared"—it is all so gloriously rich!

Change

But that glorious grace of God that brings salvation to people has lifestyle consequences for them. It cannot be otherwise! People were created in the beginning to image God (Gen 1:26–28), and so reflect to any observer what God was like. With the fall into sin people joined Satan, and so imaged the devil instead of God, reflecting to all what Satan was like (see John 8:44). As Paul put it elsewhere: "you were dead in trespasses and sins in which you once walked, following the course of this world, following the prince of the power of the air"—that is Satan (Eph 2:1–2). Restoration to God, though, means that sinners no longer reflect what Satan is like, but again image God. That is why Paul can describe for Titus the blessed consequence of Christ's victory with these words: Christ "gave himself . . . to purify for himself a people for his own possession who are zealous for good works" (Titus 2:14). Through his Holy Spirit the triumphant Savior trains sinners "to renounce ungodliness and worldly passions, and to live self-controlled, upright, and godly lives in the present age" (2:12). Even folk like the Cretans, "always liars, evil beasts, lazy gluttons" (1:12) can be changed through the mighty work of Jesus Christ; such is the culture-changing power of the gospel of redemption!

"For"

This culture-changing power of the gospel is precisely the reason why Paul would have Titus "teach . . . sound doctrine" to the older men, the older women, the young women, the younger men and the slaves. Titus 2:11–14 begins with that pivotal word "for." With that word Paul indicates that what he writes here forms the reason why he gave the instruction of the previous verses. Titus must set forth the particular task God has given to older men, older women, young women, younger men, and slaves *because* "the grace of God has appeared." History, in other words, has progressed inasmuch as God has fulfilled Old Testament prophecy in sending his Son into the world (Christmas), and this Son has triumphed on the cross so as to reconcile sinners to God (Good Friday, Easter).

It is not that older men, older women, younger women, younger men, and slaves had no role to play in maintaining and promoting spiritual health within Old Testament Israel; previous chapters have shown the contrary. Instead, the progress in redemptive history indicates that there is now greater catalyst than there ever was for these various groupings in the congregation to play their part eagerly and confidently. If we have *seen* the grace of God in Jesus Christ (and what else does "has appeared" mean), and if *we have* received salvation (and what else does "bringing salvation for all people" mean), then every congregation member of whatever rank or standing cannot but get enthusiastic about what God has done and eagerly do one's part for mutual edification. This progress in redemptive history means that Christians are on the winning team so that one day typical Cretan culture *will be no more.* The Christ who once "appeared" (2:11) will appear again in glory (2:13). On that day every trace of sin will disappear from Crete, including the "lawlessness" that yet remains within the redeemed Christian. Yes, it is catalyst for every age and social grouping amongst God's people to show themselves "zealous for good works" (2:14).

Already Covered

What, specifically, does the reference in 2:12 to renouncing "ungodliness and worldly passions" look like? And what does living "self-controlled, upright, and godly lives in the present age" look like? These terms appear directly after Paul told Titus what he had to teach the older men, the older women, the young women, the younger men, and the slaves of Crete. It is *these people*, then, who need first of all to follow through with this instruction in the actual circumstances of their daily lives. In chapters 4–8 above we already drew out how the various groupings among the Cretan Christians had to change to conform to the demands of the gospel, and we did that with repeated references to the instruction of Titus 2:12 "to renounce ungodliness and worldly passions, and to live self-controlled, upright, and godly lives in the present age." We need not repeat that material now.

Conclusion on Titus 2

Much has been written in the last number of years about the need to do home mission work, or evangelism, with pointers offered on how to do it or how to do it better. Often we end up feeling guilty that we do not do enough in this area. It is sobering, then, to realize that we search the Bible in vain for a manual on how to do home mission. Instead, there is Paul's instruction to Titus on the "sound doctrine" he has to "teach" in order to promote healthy church life in Crete:

- Older men have a task with respect to the younger men,
- Older women have a task in relation to younger women,
- Young women have a role to play in marriage and family,
- Younger men must reckon with Christ's victory over sin and Satan as they make decisions and carry out their responsibilities,

- Slaves are to adorn their service to their earthly masters with an attitude and conduct that pleases God and hence is favorable to other people.

The motive for carrying out these tasks lies in the victory of Jesus Christ on the cross, whereby sinners have been redeemed "from all lawlessness" to be a "people . . . zealous for good works."

Cretan society saw the behavior of these various groups within their midst, especially that of the more mobile and less conservative younger generation. That is why Paul concluded his instruction concerning the "young women" with the warning "that the word of God may not be reviled" (2:5b) and his instruction to "younger men" with the reminder that "an opponent may be put to shame, having nothing evil to say about us" (2:8b). Again, the slaves of the island rubbed shoulders on a daily basis with the people of town, and so Paul emphatically instructed them to "adorn the doctrine of God our Savior" (2:10b). This, surely, is as close to a home mission manual as one will get!

Today

Paul's instruction remains valid for every age group or social ranking in the church today. As Christians live out our daily calling—whether in the home or in the work force—we need to be aware of our calling to showcase the gospel. How, then, do "they" see *you*? Your attitude with which you do your daily work or run your family or involve yourself with your neighbors is of paramount importance for home missions. One can throw thousands of dollars into home mission projects (and foreign mission projects too), but it is ultimately a waste if the average person of the congregation does not illustrate to the average resident of town how great a privilege it is to be the possession of our gracious Master Jesus Christ.

That, then, is the heart of the matter: in whatever culture or circumstance I live, I am a slave of Jesus Christ, my only Master. So I do my best to be an obedient "slave of God" (1:1), in daily life, to him who saved me. *That* attitude speaks loudly to those around us—and helps to make the church of Jesus Christ function as it ought.

Paul's closing words to Titus in this chapter ring one more time in our ears: "declare these things; exhort and rebuke with all authority. Let no one disregard you" (2:15).

POINTS FOR DISCUSSION

1. The critical word in the passage under discussion is the word "for." Refresh how the material of Titus 2:11–14 impacted what the Apostle wants Titus to teach

   a. The older men,

   b. The older women,

   c. The young women,

   d. The younger men,

   e. The slaves.

2. Evangelism is a current topic in today's Christian world. How does Paul's letter to Titus give us instruction on how to go about evangelizing? What have you learned on the matter as it pertains to yourself as an older or younger person, or as an employee and perhaps as employer?

3. The preacher in your midst is mandated, like Titus was, to "declare these things; exhort and rebuke with all authority," and to permit no one to disregard him.

   a. Do you have (high) regard for your preacher or do you disregard him? Explain why you answer as you do.

   b. The longer he labors in your midst, the more you will see his weaknesses—and be tempted to trip over them. What can you do to avoid being irritated by his weaknesses? In fact, how can you obey the instruction implicit in Titus 2:15 never to "disregard" him?

   c. How can you help him to be ever more effective in the work to which God has called him?

4. If you are the preacher: how do you go about ensuring that no one disregards you?

5. If you have any other role in the church not listed in the categories mentioned above, how do you go about contributing to building up your church?

Chapter 11

In the Eye of the Public

THE APOSTLE HAD TOLD Titus in 2:1 to "teach what accords with sound doctrine." The people he was to teach were the older men (2:2), the older women (2:3) and through them the young women (2:4, 5), the younger men (2:6–8), and the slaves (2:9, 10). The reason these different age groups and social rankings in the congregation were to behave in the manner taught was that "the grace of God has appeared" (2:11–14). In the present section of his letter (3:1–8) Paul instructs Titus to address the very same audiences as were mentioned in chapter 2: "Remind *them*" (3:1). He writes:

> 3 Remind them to be submissive to rulers and authorities, to be obedient, to be ready for every good work, 2 to speak evil of no one, to avoid quarreling, to be gentle, and to show perfect courtesy toward all people. 3 For we ourselves were once foolish, disobedient, led astray, slaves to various passions and pleasures, passing our days in malice and envy, hated by others and hating one another. 4 But when the goodness and loving kindness of God our Savior appeared, 5 he saved us, not because of works done by us in righteousness, but according to his own mercy, by the washing of regeneration and renewal of the Holy Spirit, 6 whom he poured out on us richly through Jesus Christ our Savior, 7 so that being justified by his grace we might become heirs according to the

hope of eternal life. 8 The saying is trustworthy, and I want you to insist on these things, so that those who have believed in God may be careful to devote themselves to good works. These things are excellent and profitable for people.

In the passage before us now, Paul wants Titus to impress on Cretan Christians that they need always to be aware that they live in the public eye and for the public good. Submission to rulers and authorities (3:1) describes what one does in public, speaking evil of no one (3:2) refers to conversations among the public, and showing perfect courtesy toward all people (3:2) again describes the Christian's interaction with the community at large. Again, the good works the Christian does have an effect on all people (3:8).

This emphasis on the public nature of the Christian life is not new. By definition one lives in a context, and God has placed Christians of Crete deliberately in the middle of Cretan civilization. Young women were to be trained to act in a specific way "that the word of God may not be reviled" (2:5)—obviously within the general community. Titus himself needed to set a particular example among the younger men of the church "so that an opponent may be put to shame, having nothing evil to say about us" (2:8)—and the opponent certainly includes those of the community hostile to the gospel. Slaves were to "adorn the doctrine of God our Savior" through their manner of serving (2:10)—and that adorning was obviously intended for public viewing. Despite earlier hints at the need to be conscious of the public eye, Paul goes out of his way in the present paragraph to have the whole congregation instructed about the fact that each Christian always needs to be conscious of their public profile. The matter is so important that Paul tells Titus "to insist on these things" because doing good works "are excellent and profitable for people" (3:8).

Doing Good: Impossible Challenge?

The Apostle is insistent: the believers of Crete are to "be careful to devote themselves to good works" (3:8). To appreciate what Paul is driving at here, we do well to refresh ourselves first about the nature of Cretan society. In what context was Titus to insist on such behavior?

We recall from Titus 1:12 that Cretans were neither industrious nor honest; on the contrary, they habitually lied, ripped others off for their own advantage, and were gluttonous couch potatoes too lazy to move. So Paul could describe them as big mouths and leeches on society (1:10). In the paragraph now under consideration, Paul gives ugly texture to this depravity when he says of the island's Christians that "we ourselves were once foolish, disobedient, led astray, slaves to various passions and pleasures, passing our days in malice and envy, hated by others and hating one another" (3:3). It is in truth a very negative and critical presentation of the Cretans. It was well known in the world of Paul's day that in political and private dealings no one was as devious and crooked as the people of Crete.[1]

Yet Paul would not want to say that the Cretans were worse than any other people. It is not without significance that Paul included himself ("we ourselves") as he described the ugly texture of Cretan depravity. One may think here of how the Apostle before his conversion, in misdirected zeal for God, persecuted those who followed the Way (Acts 9:2). Paul had also learned from God's Old Testament revelation what God's own assessment of all humanity was. Before the great flood "the Lord saw that the wickedness of man was great in the earth, and that every intention of the thoughts of his heart was only evil continually" (Gen 6:5) so that God "blotted out every living thing that was on the face of the ground, man and animals," regardless of age (Gen 7:23). Humanity after the flood would be no better; the Lord God observed that "the intention of man's heart [remains] evil from his youth" (Gen 8:21b). It is a tragic truism valid for every tribe and race: "the heart is deceitful above all things, and desperately sick; who can understand it?" (Jer 17:9). How, one wonders, could Paul then ever instruct Titus to "insist" that Cretan Christians were to "be

---

1. See above, p. 26.

careful to devote themselves to good works"? The challenge was surely impossible!

The difficulty of the challenge becomes more apparent as one considers the details of the good works the Christians were to do. Paul mentions the following.

Submissive

"Be submissive to rulers and authorities" (3:1). Roman emperors hardly attracted respect. These emperors were largely exceedingly selfish and lived a lifestyle boasting of "ungodliness and worldly passions" (2:12). Nero, for example, was known for his homosexual activity and for preying on boys. Given such examples from the men at the top of the ladder, it is no surprise that the general population lived and tolerated lifestyles similarly offensive to the Lord God. Christians meanwhile awaited "the appearing of the glory of our great God and Savior Jesus Christ," Lord of lords and King of kings. Given his absolute authority, should Christians "be submissive to rulers and authorities," especially the ungodly ones?

Paul says "yes." He offers Titus no explanation as to why Christians were to be submissive to rulers and authorities, yet the reason is surely clear from God's earlier revelation: God alone is King (see Ps 99:1), more, Jesus Christ has triumphed over sin and Satan, has ascended into heaven and there received the throne over the universe (Acts 2:36). It follows that authorities on earth govern not by people's initiative, but are ultimately tools in his service (as Paul also says in Romans 13:1–7). Any outsider listening in on Paul's instruction here to Titus can recognize that this is basic Christian teaching. For that very reason Titus was to remind every Christian in Crete to adopt an attitude consistent with this biblical teaching, irrespective of whether the authorities—on the island or overseas—were considerate or were brutes.

Obedient

One demonstrates one's submission to rulers by ready obedience to the laws these authorities adopt. The public sees whether one obeys traffic rules, fire regulations, business law, tax law, etc. Obedience, then, is the daily face of "submission." Of course, such obedience is distinctly difficult in a society characterized by selfishness and insubordination (1:10, 12). But that is exactly Paul's point: Christians are a changed people (2:14), and so must be different to the point of sticking out.

Ready for Every Good Work

God is mighty to pull his people out of society and place them in isolation. He did not do so. The Promised Land Israel received was not a forgotten island in the world's backwater, but was located on the trade routes between the continents of Asia, Africa, and Europe. Jeremiah told the exiles in Babylon to "seek the welfare of the city where I have sent you into exile" (Jer 29:7). In keeping with God's plan the Christians of Crete continued to rub shoulders with average Cretan society, and so had to be ready to do any good work for which the Lord God gave opportunity. As Jesus put it: "Love your enemies and pray for those who persecute you, so that you may be sons of your Father who is in heaven. For he makes his sun rise on the evil and on the good, and sends rain on the just and on the unjust" (Matt 5:44–45). Though a command to love and do good was challenging in the Cretan context, such behavior was the necessary consequence of being on the receiving end of God's good work in Jesus Christ.

Speak Evil of No One

The point of Paul's instruction here is that a Christian is not to say anything that harms another's reputation—be that person a fellow believer in the church, or a fellow citizen in the community at large. This instruction again contrasts the Christian with the people of the island; they, after all, were "always liars, evil beasts" (Titus 1:12), habitually "hating one another" (3:3b). Yet precisely that behavior was condemned in the Old Testament. Think, for example, of all that is caught in the ninth commandment: "You shall not bear false witness against your neighbor" (Exod 20:16). Solomon puts the matter like this: "Whoever belittles his neighbor lacks sense, but a man of understanding remains silent. Whoever goes about slandering reveals secrets, but he who is trustworthy in spirit keeps a thing covered" (Prov 11:12–13). God himself did not speak evil of sinners, but sent his only Son for their redemption (John 3:16). Despite the difficulty of the challenge, this was the will of the Lord for his people.

Avoid Quarreling

The term Paul uses translates literally as "be non-fighting." The Apostle knew that God claimed vengeance as *his* department (Gen 12:3; Deut 32:35), knew too Jesus' instruction to "not resist the one who is evil" but to "turn to him the other" cheek (Matt 5:39), and knew also that Jesus had followed precisely this instruction when he was abused (1 Pet 2:23). It is obvious to us that anyone who chose to "be non-fighting" (be it with fists or with words) would again stick out as different—and in fact even weak.

Gentle

Paul would have the redeemed be considerate of the neighbor's needs. Instead of insisting on cold justice in the face of receiving a wrong, Paul would have the Cretan Christians pour out mercy—even upon those picking a fight with them. In practice this would mean that they would refrain from listing every wrong they see in others, and even choose not to see those wrongs. Instead, they would recognize weaknesses in themselves and respond with gentleness when another drew their attention to their weaknesses. This, of course, reflects Jesus' instruction: "So whatever you wish that others would do to you, do also to them, for this is the Law and the Prophets" (Matt 7:12). This sort of mercy mirrors God's own example in extending grace to sinners in Jesus Christ (Titus 2:11). One can well imagine how folk in Crete would snarl at each other and tear strips off the other (see 1:12; 3:3). How different the Christian was as he quit that pervasive habit!

Perfect Courtesy

The texture of these six characteristics receives further definition by the closing words of this first sentence (distinguished in Greek by a participle): "and to show perfect courtesy toward all people." The term "courtesy" captures the notion of *humility*, not in the sense of being a doormat, but in the sense of doing the right thing without consideration of personal needs. Moses was "very meek" (Num 12:3); he habitually removed himself and his personal wishes from the equation. Jesus declared "blessed" those who are "meek" (Matt 5:5) and again the point is that the meek (like Jesus) "do nothing from rivalry or conceit, but in humility count others more significant than yourselves" (Phil 2:3). Again, given typical Cretan behavior, inherently selfish as it was, the Christian's lifestyle was to be distinctly *different*, exemplifying in so many ways the attitude that marked the way Jesus Christ lived in his context of Jewish unbelief and hostility.

All this instruction about particular behavior is summed up in the words of Titus 3:8b: "I want you to insist on these things, so that those who have believed in God may be careful to devote themselves to good works." Doing good works *must* characterize the believer, irrespective of the response of the people around you. That response can be ridicule, so that the temptation is great to avoid doing good works; who, after all, wants to stick out as un-Cretan, as the duck among the chickens? But Paul is adamant; Titus must "insist on these things" (3:8). That instruction raises the question for us: *why* must Titus demand that each Christian in Crete act in a way that puts him out of step with what society considers acceptable behavior? Will insistence that Christians be different not cause (new) Christians to turn their backs on the gospel? Will it not even make the gospel unacceptable to new converts?

Why Do Good?

Titus 3:3 is connected to the previous two verses with the critical word "for." With that one little word, Paul informs his readers that what follows *gives the reason* for the command to produce outstanding public behavior. What is that reason?

The Christians of Crete used to be the way many Cretans still were: "we ourselves were once foolish, disobedient, led astray, slaves to various passions and pleasures, passing our days in malice and envy, hated by others and hating one another"—as the remainder of verse 3 says. In sharp contrast to that style of behavior, though, is God's conduct to them: "but when the goodness and loving kindness of God our Savior appeared, he saved us." The reference here is to Christmas, when God sent his Son into this world of selfish sinners. The catalyst for sending his Son was "not because of works done by us in righteousness"—as if sinners might deserve such a gift; no, "we" were doing the stuff of 3:3: being foolish, disobedient, addicted to passions and pleasures, hated and hating. Rather, the reason for sending his Son to save was simply God's "goodness" and "loving kindness" (3:4a) and "mercy" (3:5b). God was simply gracious to "liars, evil beasts, lazy gluttons" (1:12). How wonderful to be on the receiving end of such kindness!

And observe the result: "he saved us" (3:5) from that lifestyle of hateful, spiteful, disgusting, selfish passions that led to civil war, to consuming each other. See 3:5b: he saved us "by the washing of regeneration and renewal of the Holy Spirit"—terms that describe *change* in lifestyle so that we are now no longer what we "were once" (3:3).

The radical nature of the Spirit's renewing work is illustrated in the biblical record of what happened on the day of Pentecost. People who seven weeks earlier cried out to "crucify, crucify him" (Luke 23:21) were so changed by the Spirit of Pentecost that "they were selling their possessions and belongings and distributing the proceeds to all, as any had need" (Acts 2:45). The selfishness, evil passions, and hating that used to characterize them (and which still characterized the unbelieving of Crete) was replaced by the kindness and love and mercy of God as he had displayed it in Jesus Christ. These sinners were changed to image God again (Gen 1:26–28)!

The same is true of the saints of Crete. Because of the renewing work of the Holy Spirit they are no longer what they *used to be*: "foolish, disobedient, led astray, slaves to various passions and pleasures" (3:3). Since they were now changed, they were "justified by his grace" and "heirs according to the hope of eternal life" (3:7). Truly, the gospel is glorious!

These Cretan believers needed now to act in a fashion consistent with the change the Lord God had worked in their hearts. They were, in other words, to be as good and gracious and merciful to others as God manifestly had been to them in sending his Son for their salvation. Titus' task was to "remind them . . . to be ready for every good work . . . to be gentle, and to show perfect courtesy toward all people" (3:1, 2)—and so reflect what God was like.

The Word Is Faithful!

One can appreciate that the challenge given here to Titus is enormous. In the island's ungodliness, Titus must "insist" (3:8) on that lifestyle characterized by "good works." Is there any encouragement for him?

Yes, there is. Before the Apostle tells Titus to "insist on these things," he reminds his reader that "the Word is faithful" (3:8a).[2] Common English translations, however, render the Greek phrase πιστὸς ὁ λόγος variously, as the following table illustrates:

---

2. Paul uses the same phrase a total of five times in the Pastoral Epistles, viz., 1 Tim 1:15; 3:1; 4:9; 2 Tim 2:11; and Titus 3:8. The various English translations do not all translate the phrase consistently in each instance.

King James Version	This is a faithful saying
New American Standard Version	This is a trustworthy saying
Revised Standard Version	The saying is sure
New King James Version	This is a faithful saying
English Standard Version	The saying is trustworthy
New International Version	This is a trustworthy saying

In the translations listed above, the word λόγος is repeatedly rendered with the English term "saying." The terms "faithful," "trustworthy" and "sure" come down to the same thing (as translation of πιστός), so that on this term too there is agreement in translation.[3] Where the translations differ is that some use the word "the" while others use the word "this." That is because commentators largely agree that Paul is claiming that the particular statement (or saying) that he is quoting (or has just written) is actually faithful, trustworthy, sure.

The problem here is twofold. In the first place, the plain translation of the Greek is "the word is faithful," and not "*this* word is faithful" or "*this* is a faithful word." Elsewhere in this letter (and in his other epistles too) Paul uses the word λόγος to refer to the gospel itself (e.g., Titus 1:3 and 2:9). That word (that is, the gospel) is faithful, reliable, trustworthy—which is why Paul was charged to preach it (1:3) and why Paul also wants Titus to teach it. In the second place, if we are to think that every time Paul uses this phrase he is referring to a particular "saying" he is quoting, then we are left with the need to find that saying somewhere in the proximity of where he uses the phrase. But that becomes artificial. To stay with the passage currently under discussion: what might the "saying" be that Paul is referring to when he says in 3:8a: "the saying is faithful"? Is he referring to the entirety of 3:4–7? But that is hardly a "saying"![4]

3. The differences in word order do not change the meaning of the various translations.

4. The same challenge arises in other places where Paul uses the phrase, as listed in footnote 2. Only in 1 Timothy 1:15 could one possibly maintain

If, on the other hand, we stay with the straightforward meaning of the Greek, we can understand the phrase as an exclamation of Paul's confidence in the Word (i.e., the gospel), a confidence Paul wants to share with Titus. Titus, we had noted earlier, faced a difficult task in Crete inasmuch as he had the mandate to "insist" that the Christians of the island behave in a pattern distinctly different from normal Cretan behavior. *Insisting* that Christians devote themselves to good works would surely complicate Titus' mandate on the island, and so demoralize him; who, after all, wants to be different from the crowds! Paul's encouragement is plain: "the Word is faithful!" That Word tells us of how God in kindness has given his Son to redeem sinners, and how he also has given his Holy Spirit to regenerate his own, so that sinners are made heirs of life eternal (3:4–7). The Word is not false in what it says about God's grace in Jesus Christ and about Christ's victory over sin and Satan. "The Word is faithful," trustworthy, sure—and so sinful Cretan society cannot and will not have the last word.

Here, then, is great encouragement for Titus in the challenges he faces in Crete. Because of Christmas and Good Friday redemption is reality, and so Titus must preach the gospel of God's grace, kindness, mercy, and *insist* that the congregation act consistently with God's mighty work in Jesus Christ as they go about their daily affairs in the community. Was it tough for Titus to insist on good works? Was it awkward for Cretan Christians to be just as gracious, just as kind and just as merciful to undeserving brutes around them as God was to them? Undoubtedly. But the Word is faithful, the Gospel is true, and so what it says about how sin-filled hearts are changed is a delightful reality. The question is not whether you think the challenge to live Christianly is too hard; the question is rather whether you *believe* the glorious reality of what the Word accomplishes.

---

that Paul is referring to a saying he has just quoted (1:15b). But commentators struggle to find the saying he could be referring to in the other passages.

Consequence

What, we wonder, might the impact of Titus' preaching have been on the Christians of Crete? How did Titus' insistence on good works help complete the work Paul had left unfinished in Crete? The Holy Spirit has not revealed to us the answer to that question. Perhaps that is because our emphasis should not be on what the fruits of Titus' labors in Crete may have been, but ought instead to be on what fruit there is in our own lives and midst today as we digest the same word the Cretan Christians received. Our culture, after all, is not essentially different from that of Crete two thousand years ago. It takes much courage on our part to devote ourselves to good works, being submissive to our rulers and authorities, being obedient in a disobedient environment, being ready for every good work in an apostate society, speaking evil of no one even as others around us speak evil of another (and of Christians in particular), etc.

It is a challenge, but the challenge is not too hard; "the Word is faithful!" Apostasy will not have the last word! Through the genuine witness of those redeemed by Jesus' blood and renewed by his Spirit, the Lord's church building work is advanced—whether on the island of Crete or in our nation today.

POINTS FOR DISCUSSION

1. The Cretans were distinctly ungodly in their lifestyle, according to Titus 3:3. Their basic behavior was at heart the same as that of the people before the Great Flood.

    a. Find other passages in the Scriptures Paul used that show how depraved the human heart actually is.

    b. Would you say that people have become better over the centuries? Do you see yourself and your loved ones as similar to the people of Noah's days and the people of Crete? Why or why not?

2. Titus must teach the people of Crete to "be submissive to rulers and authorities." Do some research on the rulers and authorities of Titus' day. Would you still think it necessary to "be submissive" to those men? Why or why not? What does that teach us about how the Lord would have us think, speak and act in relation to those who rule over us today?

3. Are you "ready for every good work" in your community? How does your community read your willingness? Are there changes you can or should make here?

4. Why is it necessary for the Christian "to speak evil of no one," "to avoid quarreling," "to be gentle," and "to show perfect courtesy toward all people"? Does your community see you living in obedience to this instruction? Does your community see your church walking in obedience to this instruction? Explain why you answer as you do.

5. What is the meaning of the phrase translated as "the saying is trustworthy" in Titus 3:8? What encouragement does this phrase have for

   a. The preacher?

   b. The hearer of the gospel?

6. The Holy Spirit has not told us how the Cretan Christians responded to Titus' efforts to teach them the material of Paul's letter to him.

   a. What can we learn from the fact that the Holy Spirit has not told us?

   b. What has changed in your life as a result of listening to Paul's letter to Titus?

   c. To the preacher: How has your congregation changed as a result of this letter?

Chapter 12

Avoiding Foolish Controversies

PAUL HAD LEFT TITUS on the island of Crete with a twofold assignment: First, to appoint elders in every town, and second to teach what accords with sound doctrine in relation to various age and social groups among the believers. The former task was largely a one-time assignment, while the latter task required ongoing work.[1] As a final word to Titus on this ongoing aspect of his assignment (3:9–11), Paul gives this instruction:

> 9 But avoid foolish controversies, genealogies, dissensions, and quarrels about the law, for they are unprofitable and worthless. 10 As for a person who stirs up division, after warning him once and then twice, have nothing more to do with him, 11 knowing that such a person is warped and sinful; he is self-condemned.

Paul, it appears, was confident that Titus, his "true child in a common faith" (1:4), would present the gospel faithfully. Human as he was, though, Titus could easily be distracted from his task, especially in a culture where the works of the flesh dominated so thoroughly as they did in Crete. It is to that possibility that Paul

---

1. The verb rendered as "appoint" in 1:5 is in the aorist tense, indicating one-time action. The verbs "teach" in 2:1, "declare," "exhort," and "rebuke" in 2:15, "remind" in 3:1, and "insist" in 3:8 are all in the present tense, indicating ongoing action.

now turns. He draws to Titus' attention what means Satan would use to distract the preacher, and what the preacher is to do about it.

The Danger of Distraction

Any preacher—Titus included—is vulnerable to outside pressures. The fact is that there are forceful people around, folk—perhaps well intentioned, perhaps not—who raise side issues or make statements that direct the preacher down an unnecessary rabbit trail. In the Cretan culture of lying and laziness there were "many who are insubordinate, empty talkers and deceivers" (1:10). What would it take for Titus to get tangled up in that empty talk—so that what is edifying gets forgotten? Hence Paul's pointed instruction to Titus: "avoid foolish controversies, genealogies, dissensions, and quarrels about the law" (3:9).

Controversies

The term "controversies" is a derivative of the Greek word meaning "to seek." Before you can *find* answers you need the right attitude, that is, you need to be *seeking* to learn—and therefore are eager to listen. But in this case the "seeking" is "foolish," stupid. The picture generated by the use of the word "controversies" is that of a person asking questions without really wanting the answer; he has his rejoinder ready well before the answer is out. Perhaps his mind is already made up, or perhaps he is not really interested in the answer. Perhaps he would rather debate for the sheer challenge of the debate rather than for the sake of finding solid answers. Whatever the case, the net effect on Titus is clear: his time is wasted and his energy is burnt. To the degree that Titus gets himself involved in such a debate he is not giving himself to his mandate to "teach what accords with sound doctrine" (2:1). Hence Paul's instruction: "avoid foolish controversies."

What kind of controversies might these be? Records have been discovered from the time of the early church demonstrating that intense discussions were held on whether angels were circumcised. In the Middle Ages lengthy debates were held on how many angels could dance on the head of a needle. We well understand that one can scour Scripture, logic, science, and so many other sources for arguments to make one's position more credible than the opponents' position, and even expend endless energy and hours on the effort. But issues as these obviously do not help in the practical questions of real life, and do not contribute to the wellbeing of the Lord's church. On the contrary, such controversies are simply foolish.

Genealogies

The Apostle urged Titus also to avoid "genealogies." The term appears to refer to pulling names from the genealogies scattered throughout the Old Testament, and then extracting wisdom and lessons from the mere mention of a name. Perhaps it is not unlike palm reading or horoscopes in our day. "Genealogies," in other words, involved pure speculation. And with speculation, of course, human thought takes precedence over divine revelation. Such speculation is foolish and unhelpful—but the fact of the matter is that some can get really heated on it, and become convinced of their conclusions too. Titus must again avoid involvement in such discussions because he must stay focused on his task of completing his assignment—appointing elders and teaching sound doctrine.

Dissensions

Paul also mentions "dissensions." This reference is to disagreements that drive a wedge between brothers in the faith. It is easily done. A notable issue in my childhood was whether a woman was permitted to wear pants in a social setting. Some years later a point of dissension was how long a man's hair should be. More recently there has been debate on whether there should be alcohol in the drink used at the Lord's Supper. To defend that women could wear pants meant you were liberal, and therefore written off by certain stalwarts of the faith. To claim that it was acceptable for a man to have long hair meant you were worldly and therefore not trustworthy. What you thought on the subject of how much alcohol there should be in the Lord's Supper wine indicated whether you were truly reformed or not, or perhaps how sensitive you were to others' struggles. Though such issues may have merit in themselves, Paul tells Titus (and so every leader) that it is not helpful to pronounce on an answer. Getting embroiled in such matters detracts from the time and energy, not to mention credibility, needed to advance the gospel.

Quarrels about the Law

Titus is also to "avoid . . . quarrels about the law." The term "law" describes the first portion of the Scripture the church in Paul's day had, namely, the five books of Moses. It is unclear what matters of "the law" were quarreled about, but it is certainly clear what effect quarreling about the law would have on society's perception of Christians and their Scripture. In his task of building up church life in Crete, Titus needed to avoid getting caught up in quarrels about any passage of Scripture. Quarreling on the interpretation of, say, Genesis 1 or Leviticus 13 or any other portion of the Torah would not only drain Titus' energy, but would ultimately send the signal that God's Word is not clear. Such fogginess undermines the Bible's authority.

Avoid

It is not so hard to muster arguments for any given position, or even to build up an entire theology to make the issue sound vital to the future of the church. One can elevate any matter to be *the* mark of whether the church is reforming or apostatizing. That is especially so in a culture of lazy windbags who loved to talk, stir the pot, and foment trouble (cf. Titus 1:10, 12), where "their consciences are defiled" and they do not know God (1:15–16). Even Christians are not above such works of the flesh (Gal 5:20).

But Titus must studiously avoid any involvement in such talk, discussions, controversies and arguments because they are "unprofitable and worthless" in achieving Titus' goal of promoting church life in Crete.

Teach

What is Titus to do instead? He is to "*teach* what accords with sound doctrine" (2:1), is to "*declare* these things; *exhort* and *rebuke* with all authority" (2:15), is to "*remind*" (3:1) and is to "*insist* on these things" (3:8). The instruction to "insist on these things" appears directly before the instruction to "avoid foolish controversies" and so gets to the heart of why Titus must "avoid."

For the benefit of people embroiled in their foolishness and sinfulness, God displayed his delightful "goodness and loving kindness" (3:4) in that he sent his Son into this world to be "our Savior" (3:4), through whom "he saved us . . . according to his own mercy" (3:5). The blessed result is that sinners are "justified by his grace" and have "become heirs according to the hope of eternal life" (3:7).

Given such exciting and stimulating gospel, shall Titus allow himself to get sidetracked by debates on whether angels are circumcised, or who should wear pants on what occasion, or how much alcohol there should be in the Lord's Supper cup? Let Titus preach the Word and so ensure that the congregation's heads are filled with the glories of the gospel—so that in turn there be no oxygen left upon which foolish controversies and arguments might thrive. "These things are excellent and profitable for people" (3:8c), while controversies are "unprofitable" (3:9c).

The picture, then, is clear. If any preacher lets himself get distracted by issues, he simply will not be able to keep directing his congregation to the delightful gospel of God's goodness in Jesus Christ. As long as the congregation's eye (and his own) is off the glory of the Savior, controversies will grow, issues will gain a life of their own, the church will become a hotbed of dissension, and brother will eventually rise against brother until there comes a parting of ways. Jesus' warning is to the point: "Every kingdom divided against itself is laid waste, and no city or house divided against itself will stand" (Matt 12:25). Controversies do not build up the church of Jesus Christ, but tear her apart. So Titus in Crete—and every preacher anywhere in the world—needs to avoid controversies, and persist in preaching the gospel of the appearing of the goodness and loving kindness of God in Jesus Christ. "Insist on these things" (Titus 3:8).

Treatment of Distractors

Though Titus is not to get caught up in the controversies and quarrels that arise, he is at the same time not to ignore those who fuel the controversies. Instead, the Apostle gives his associate in Crete specific instructions in relation to the "person who stirs up division" between brothers. Writes Paul: "As for a person who stirs up division, after warning him once and then twice, have nothing more to do with him, knowing that such a person is warped and sinful; he is self-condemned" (3:10–11).

Nothing More to Do with Him

It is tempting to understand the phrase "have nothing more to do with him" as a reference to excommunication, so that Paul here tells Titus to cut such persons off from the fledging church on the island. It is questionable, however, whether that is the right understanding of the phrase. Consider the following thoughts:

- In his letter to Titus Paul is giving instructions to Titus alone, and not to the body of elders. Admittedly, elders and others through the ages can learn much from what Paul writes to Titus, but the fact remains that Paul wrote this letter with one addressee in mind. But Titus himself could not excommunicate a member on his own. When Jesus outlined what was to happen to a sinning brother, he stipulated that his transgression (and what had been done about it) was to be reported to the *church* (Matt 18:17). Paul himself, with apostolic authority, told the *church* in Corinth to "deliver [the sinner] to Satan"; he did not presume to do the excommunication himself (1 Cor 5:5). Titus could not excommunicate an errant member on his own.

- The term here translated as "have nothing . . . to do (with him)" has the sense of "repudiate," "spurn." The instruction then is that Titus is to *walk around* the divisive man, stay away from him. Neither in public nor in private is Titus to engage this brother in discussions as long as the conversation would be nothing else than worthless debate.

It is not that Titus is to deny the divisive brother any explanation for why he avoids him. Paul stipulates that Titus must "warn him once and then twice." You can see it happening in the eye of your mind: Titus and a brother of the congregation end up in conversation and the brother turns the conversation to his pet topic to hear what Pastor Titus thinks about it—not with a view to learning from Titus, but instead to determine the pastor's orthodoxy or to bolster his own self-esteem or to impress a third party on his own knowledge. I would imagine that Titus could fulfill Paul's instruction by explaining to his conversation partner that the discussion has taken a turn that does not edify, and so declining further dialogue. It may well be that the divisive brother does not see himself as divisive. Titus, then, is to admonish him in love and make clear that the matter with which he busies his mind and conversation actually diverts attention away from the gospel of glory, and so is not God-glorifying; the brother needs to repent, fix his eye on God and delight in his goodness as demonstrated in Jesus Christ. That such an admonition should be made once and then a second time follows the pattern of Jesus' instruction in Matthew 18:15–16 about the double admonition.

Of course, one wants to hear that the brother concerned has acknowledged the divisiveness of dwelling on his pet peeves and repented of his sin. That, however, might not happen. In the event that he stays focused on his issues (instead of on the gospel), Titus is to steer clear of the brother altogether on grounds that this brother is "warped and sinful"—for his mind is not absorbed by the marvels of the gospel of grace.

Self-Condemned

It is a hard thing to grasp. Perhaps the brother in question still comes diligently to church, still confesses Jesus Christ as Lord, still appears faithfully at Bible study events, still serves on various church committees. Yet Paul tells Titus that this brother is "warped"; he is willfully living in a pattern of sin. The point is that he ought to have his head and his heart full of the "goodness and loving kindness of God" as he displayed it in the gift of Jesus Christ—and so contribute to growth in the Lord's church. If he is an older brother, he is to set the example to the younger; if she is an older sister, she is to get into the homes of the younger to teach; if she is a younger sister, she is to be eager to learn from the instruction of the older and then serve her husband and children; if he is a younger brother he is similarly to be keen to grow through what others have to say and show it to those for whom he is responsible; if he is a slave he is to "be well-pleasing, not argumentative." In *no* circumstance is he to ride his own hobbyhorse—and when he does he simply demonstrates that he has not grasped the glory of the gospel, even though he calls himself a Christian and keeps coming to church. He is "warped"—and the way Paul put the Greek together makes plain that this description characterizes him.[2] The result is an ongoing, persistent habit: he is living in sin.[3] Only God can straighten out what is warped, and correct those who live in sin.

2. The word "warped" is in the perfect tense, signifying that the person concerned once became warped and so now remains warped.

3. The word "sinful" is in the present tense, signifying that the person concerned is habitually sinning.

Titus, then, does not need to make a judgment on the brother. By his conduct the brother does it himself; he is *self-condemned.*

Ignored?

If Titus, then, is to "walk around" the divisive person, would Paul have the church do the same? It is important to note that Paul had earlier instructed Titus to "appoint elders in every town" (1:5), brothers of particular quality (1:6–9). The reason for doing so was caught in 1:10: "*for* there are many who are insubordinate, empty talkers." Undoubtedly their empty talk included the foolish controversies, genealogies, dissensions, and quarrels about the law Titus was to avoid. But these brothers and sisters are part of the congregation entrusted to the care of the elders Titus must appoint, and that can only mean that these elders have the task to address the divisive brother. As to Titus, nothing whatsoever is to distract him; he is to preach the gospel of Christ's triumph with no interference.

Consequence

Today's preachers repeatedly experience the same headwinds that Titus experienced in response to their work. Satan, after all, continues to do all he can to sabotage good progress in the Lord's church gathering work. The preacher, though, is to stay focused on his mandate, and permit nothing to divert him from his task.

By the same token, no believer, whether older man, older woman, younger woman, younger man, slave, or anybody else for that matter, ought to impose his pet hobbies on the preacher. Each believer needs the gospel of redemption, and so is to give the preacher the space he requires to prepare himself to "teach what accords with sound doctrine" (2:1). In fact, older men and older women do well to encourage and admonish their own generation and those who come after them to stay focused on the glories of God's goodness and loving kindness as displayed in Jesus Christ.

In the face of controversies and quarrels, such mutual encouragement to remain focused on the gospel contributes to enriching the church—for the benefit of members and community alike.

POINTS FOR DISCUSSION

1. In your circle, what means has Satan attempted to use to distract your preacher from proclaiming the gospel? What means has Satan used to hinder you from hearing and/or receiving the proclamation? Are there steps you can take to ensure this does not happen again—or does not continue to happen?

2. It is not difficult to stir up dissension. Why might that be so? What attitude does the Lord want us to adopt in the face of dissent? What does this mean for the kinds of issues you expect your preacher to address from the pulpit?

3. The interpretation of Genesis 1, the role of women in the church, the meaning of baptism, the manner of celebrating Lord's Supper, and multiple such like topics attract heated discussion amongst many Christians in today's Western world. Would Paul have Titus skirt such topics in his instruction to "avoid . . . quarrels about the law"? Why or why not? What effect do controversies on issues as these have on the credibility of the gospel? How ought your preacher to "teach . . . sound doctrine" on such topics? What mindset does the Apostle imply in this instruction on the part of congregation members?

4. Why is a person caught up in controversies "self-condemned"? Perhaps someone in your midst is pushing his own view on such issues as mentioned in the previous question. In your opinion, is it fair (or even accurate) to say of this person that he is "self-condemned," let alone "warped and sinful"? Explain why you answer as you do.

5. How is Titus to deal with those caught up in controversies? How do you deal with such persons? How does your church deal with such persons?

6. How can your elders play a helpful role in your church community in preventing or deflating controversies? Given what Paul wrote in Titus 1 about the requirements for the elder, how would you deal with an elder pushing his own pet ideas?

7. How could older men and older women play a helpful role in your church community in preventing or deflating controversies?

Chapter 13

Pulling the Preacher

WITH HIS INSTRUCTION ON the two aspects of Titus' assignment complete, the Apostle Paul is free to close off his letter. He does so with his traditional greeting (3:15). First, though, he gives to Titus the surprising directive to terminate his work on the island (3:12–14). Paul writes:

> 12 When I send Artemas or Tychicus to you, do your best to come to me at Nicopolis, for I have decided to spend the winter there. 13 Do your best to speed Zenas the lawyer and Apollos on their way; see that they lack nothing. 14 And let our people learn to devote themselves to good works, so as to help cases of urgent need, and not be unfruitful.

We are taken aback with this instruction! As we looked over Titus' shoulder as he read Paul's letter, and as we observe Titus reflecting on what his teaching needs to sound like, we imagine weeks of hard work stacked up in front of him. To complete what is yet unfinished in Crete—there is so much for Titus to do! But now, as Titus is about to get at it, he gets told to pack his bags!

Questions arise in our minds. Why does Paul want Titus to leave Crete now? Is departure in fact responsible? Further questions bubble up: What is the connection between the instruction to travel to Nicopolis (3:12) and the instruction to speed Zenas and

Apollos on their way (3:13)? Is the command to "let our people learn to devote themselves to good works" (3:14) connected in any way to the instruction to travel to Nicopolis (3:12) and to speed Zenas and Apollos on their way (3:13)? How does the material of this paragraph connect to the instructions Paul had earlier given to Titus?

Paul's Surprising Instruction

It is likely, though not certain, that Paul was in Corinth when he wrote his letter to Titus. What is certain is that Paul was anxious to carry on with his God-given task of preaching the Word to those who did not yet know Christ (Acts 9:15). But winter was approaching, and winter was not a good time to travel, whether by boat or foot. From mid-September to early March winds and rains made travel risky in the Mediterranean basin. Luke records the dangers of such travel when he recounts how Paul's ship left the security of Fair Haven's harbor en route to Rome and ended up shipwrecking on the island of Malta (see Acts 27:13–20). Paul's awareness of the risks of winter travel explains why he decided to winter in one location.

Nicopolis

The city where he determined to winter was Nicopolis. Presumably Paul is referring to the Nicopolis on the west coast of Achaia, just across the sea from the heel of Italy's boot (for the Roman world had more than one city with that name). This is an area where the Apostle had not yet preached the gospel. The city's population and connections to inland communities could serve as a good launching pad for mission work in the surrounding region, and the proximity of this port city to Italy could perhaps also make it a suitable staging place for heading off to Spain in the spring via Rome.

Paul wants Titus to join him for the winter, and so tells him to "do your best to come to me in Nicopolis" (3:12). Paul does not explain his reasons. It is, however, clear that the Apostle's wish had very serious consequences for Titus, not to mention the Christians of Crete. Paul, as we noted extensively before, had left Titus in Crete for the distinct purpose of finishing what was still incomplete in the churches on the island—and then wrote Titus specific instructions about what to do to accomplish that goal. Now *this very same letter* ends with an instruction to Titus to "come to me at Nicopolis," and the implication is clearly that Titus must *quit his work in Crete!* More, he must terminate his work on the island *not* when the work is done, but "when I send Artemas or Tychicus to you" (3:12).

Artemas and Tychicus

We know nothing about Artemas other than what is mentioned in this text. Tychicus, on the other hand, is known to be one of Paul's trusted travel companions and assistants (Acts 20:4; Eph 6:21; Col 4:7 and 2 Tim 4:12). At the time of writing, Paul had not yet decided which of these two he would send to Crete to replace Titus.

Since Crete was an island, one of these two men would invariably have to arrive by ship—just as Paul's letter would have come to the island by ship. We (and Titus) have no clue when the ship would arrive—except that winter is coming and by that time Titus is to be in Nicopolis.

Pressure!

Titus, then, has urgent work to do. *As soon as* his replacement arrives, Titus is to organize his ticket, pack his bags, and board the next ship out. Then he must cross the channel to the mainland (a distance of about two hundred kilometers) and walk to Nicopolis (another two hundred kilometers or so); alternatively he must wait for a boat that will take him directly to Nicopolis (a few hundred kilometers by sea).

We do not know the exact time frame between Titus receiving this letter and the date he must leave (i.e., when his replacement arrives). It is clear, though, that Titus does not have months; he has weeks or perhaps only days. So the window of time left for his work in Crete is rather small. The man is invariably under pressure to be as effective in his work as he can be with the remaining time.

Puzzled

To be honest, we find this development surprising. From our perspective, it is simply not convenient or timely for Titus to leave the island. He has just received detailed instructions as to what he must do among a people where "many . . . are insubordinate, empty talkers and deceivers" who "profess to know God, but . . . deny him by their works" (1:10, 16); that is why Titus had to "appoint elders" (1:5) and then had to "teach" (2:1), "declare," "exhort," "rebuke" (2:15), "remind" (3:1), and "insist" (3:8). Shall Titus *now* leave? Even if there will be a replacement, we find it hard to grasp that Titus' departure *now* is helpful to the work of the Lord on the island. Solomon put the problem well: "I hated all my toil in which I toil under the sun, seeing that I must leave it to the man who will come after me, and who knows whether he will be wise or a fool?" (Eccl 2:18–19). Further: shall those young Christians of Crete be denied any say as to when their minister leaves? Is Titus himself even allowed an opinion on the matter? The whole thing strikes us as so very insensitive, and even selfish on Paul's part.

Titus' Response

As a man of faith Titus knows very well that he, like Paul, is "a servant of God . . . for the sake of the faith of God's elect" (1:1). As a servant he needs to accept the fact that the Head of the church may move him wherever and whenever he wishes. It will not do for Titus to insist that the islanders need to submit to God's word and at the same time himself defy God's instruction as given to him through Paul. In relation to those younger than himself on the island, Titus is "to be sober-minded, dignified, self-controlled, sound in faith, in love and in steadfastness" (2:2), and as a younger man Titus is "to be a model of good works" (2:7). In a word, he must set the example of what it means to follow the Head of the church, the Lord Jesus Christ.

That means in practice that Titus is to accept Paul's seemingly selfish instruction and wrap up the work he was to do on the island. He must:

- Quickly travel to those towns of Crete where there are believers, identify specific candidates for the office of elder, and ordain them—and perhaps do some training too.

- Teach older men and women as well as younger men and slaves their respective roles in God's church. To do that task well and efficiently he must avoid "foolish controversies" (3:9).

Meanwhile, his bags are half packed, for he does not know when Artemas or Tychicus will arrive. The point is clear: there is *urgency to work hard!* Titus must preach the Word as long as the small window of opportunity remains open! God puts pressure on Titus to perform.

Hospitality

As if this pressure is not enough, Paul adds another mandate to what Titus needs to do. Paul informs Titus that two strangers have just appeared amongst the Christians of Crete, namely "Zenas the lawyer and Apollos" (3:13). We know nothing of Zenas (neither the Bible nor other literature mention him), while Apollos we know as another of Paul's coworkers (see Acts 18:24). The fact that Paul knows they have come to the island suggests they came as bearers of Paul's letter to Titus. However that may have been, they needed housing while they rested up, and then supplies for their further journey, perhaps on the next ship out.

The culture of the day did not know of hotels where one could spend the night. Further, the berth purchased on a ship did not come with blankets, nor did passage include meals; such personal niceties were one's own responsibility. So it fell to the Christians of Crete to extend hospitality to these two men for the night, and then give them whatever they needed for their further travels. Hence Paul's instruction to Titus: "Do your best to speed Zenas the lawyer and Apollos on their way; see that they lack nothing" (3:13).

Talk about pressure! Titus has but a short time left to fulfill all Paul's instructions in this letter. He was even expressly told not to get distracted by controversies (3:9), but now must get involved in the needs of two strangers. Is that not deeply contradictory?

The Love of the Gospel

No, this is not contradictory. Titus' mandate in Crete was (besides appointing elders) to "teach what accords with sound doctrine" (2:1). He had to unpack, in practical terms, what it means that "the *grace* of God has appeared, bringing salvation for all people" (2:11). Paul repeats the concept some verses later when he mentions that "the goodness and loving kindness of God our Savior appeared" (3:4). Words like "grace" and "goodness" and "loving kindness" describe what Christmas and Good Friday were about. "God so loved the world, that he gave his only Son, that whoever believes in him should not perish but have eternal life" (John 3:16). This divine love in Jesus Christ changes people so that they reflect God's style. The public *look* of the gospel must be as generous, as kind, as gracious as the Lord's own goodness and kindness. Titus as the preacher has to illustrate this gospel through his conduct. Not only must he as a young man show himself in all respects to be "a model of good works" (2:7), but he must now also dress up his preaching through specific acts of love to guests. Even if public conduct is commonly marked by reserve to strangers, Titus must demonstrate love and grace and kindness to visitors. Such conduct will empower his preaching.

We are not told how Titus responded to the urgency of the moment. Did he perform as he ought? The Holy Spirit has not told us because more important for us than Titus' response is our own response. For "the goodness and loving kindness of God our Savior appeared" (3:4) for our benefit too, so that we also have been renewed through the Holy Spirit. So it is our privilege, in the pressures of our daily obligations, to illustrate God's love in how we show hospitality to another in need. Words and deeds, faith and action are inseparable!

And the Cretans . . .

We realize that it would not be brotherly for Titus to keep to himself Paul's instruction to him to leave on the first ship after the arrival of his replacement—be that tomorrow, next week or next month. After all, the option of simply disappearing, or giving shorter notice still, is simply not acceptable.

It raises the question: how should the Christians of Crete—relatively new as they are to the faith—respond to the news that their preacher Titus is leaving? Should they get upset and frustrated because they are being left in the lurch? Should they wonder if their new faith is worth maintaining if their leaders and teachers do not (bother to) complete the task they had begun? How would we respond in a parallel situation?

The Christian faith does not depend on people, not even on men of such stature as Paul or Titus. Paul said it well in another letter he wrote: "What then is Apollos? What is Paul? Servants through whom you believed, as the Lord assigned to each. I planted, Apollos watered, but God gave the growth. So neither he who plants nor he who waters is anything, but only God who gives the growth" (1 Cor 3:5–7).

But if growth is God's sovereign activity, it does not matter which person God is pleased to use to bring about the growth—be that Paul or Titus or even Artemas or Tychicus. It will not do, then, for the Cretan Christians to get discouraged on account of Titus' departure. Their eye is to remain on the ascended Christ, their

Lord and Savior, in the confidence that Christ will complete the work that he has begun (see Ps 138:8).

At the same time, those Christians of Crete are to *do* whatever the Lord God gives them to do. As Paul writes in 3:14: "And let our people learn to devote themselves to good works." That is what Christ had done for the undeserving through his sacrifice on the cross, as Paul had emphasized so often in his letter already (cf. 2:3b; 2:14b; 3:1b; 3:8). *That* is the conduct Titus is to exemplify in his remaining days on the island. And *that* is the form of behavior the Cretan Christians need to master. Being busy with doing good is simply essential to being a Christian. It does not matter, then, whether the Master calls his "servant" Paul (1:1) or Titus to another task. *You* just do what the Lord wants *you* to do: devote yourself to doing good works, whether you be an older man, an older woman, a young woman, a younger man or even a slave—and so extend willing hospitality to folks in need like Zenas and Apollos.

Not Unfruitful

By so doing, the Apostle concludes, you "help cases of urgent need, and (will) not be unfruitful." The reference to fruitfulness recalls imagery Jesus used when he spoke about himself as the vine in John 15:5, with the disciples as the branches who drew their sap from the true vine and in turn bore fruit. Jesus, though, was snatched from the disciples long before they were ready to see him go. One could forgive the disciples for thinking that Jesus' crucifixion and death meant that the work begun in their hearts would now shrivel and perish. His return to them after his resurrection was again cut short through his ascension into heaven—and again one could forgive the disciples for thinking that Jesus' departure was bad for their growth. But it turned out so differently. Jesus in heaven labored for the disciples' advantage. More, he sent to them the Helper (John 14:16, 26; 15:26; 16:7), who equipped them richly to bring forth abundant fruit (Acts 2:4; 4:8; Gal 5:22–23). All who belong to Jesus Christ similarly bring forth delightful fruit as they give themselves to doing good works in their local circumstances.

Well then, the Christians of Crete should not despair as to what their future might hold; they should instead obediently and confidently do the good works their Lord and Savior had equipped them to do—be they elders, older men, older women, young women, younger men, or slaves. In so doing they would bear rich fruit in the church, to God's glory and their neighbor's advantage.

Conclusion

The sermon Titus was preparing at the time he received this letter from Paul may well have turned out to be the last sermon he preached on the island of Crete. That reality is conceivably true for any of us today, be it in preparing sermons, or in receiving sermons. The same is true for the opportunity to do good deeds to those around us. The Lord can easily change our circumstances tonight so that we can no longer touch the other with the good deeds we would want to do. We simply do not know today what tomorrow will bring.

That reality gives urgency to each day and to each moment. Preachers do well to preach every sermon as if it will be the last one they ever preach. Hearers do equally well to listen to every sermon as if it will be the last sermon they will ever hear. And every Christian ought to do his good deeds as if the present moment is the last chance one receives to reflect what Christ has done for the undeserving. Such conduct contributes to the progress of the Lord's church gathering work.

Points for Discussion

1. Ministers come and go. Is it acceptable to you that a successful preacher moves away before his work (in your opinion) is completed in your congregation? Explain your answer. How do you respond to his decision to move away? How does that compare to your response when a less successful preacher moves away?

2. Is it right of Paul to require that Titus leave Crete so shortly after receiving the instructions of this letter? Why would Paul give Titus the instructions he gave—only to require him to leave? What does this teach you about the importance of your preacher?

3. Titus must show Christian hospitality to "Zenas the lawyer and Apollos." How does this instruction fit into the rest of the letter? What does this instruction teach us about showing hospitality to strangers? See also Hebrews 13:2.

4. We are not told how Titus responded to the command to show hospitality, let alone whether he in fact took the next ship to Nicopolis. Is it important for us to know Titus' response? Why or why not?

5. Titus' approaching departure would invariably impact the work of elders, older men, and older women in the churches of Crete.

   a. Explore how the responsibility of each of those groupings would be affected by Titus' departure.

   b. Imagine your minister were called to serve in another congregation. How would his departure affect the work of elders, older men, and older women in your church?

   c. Would you consider it possible that your minister's departure brings out a collapse in the congregation? What can be done today to ensure that a collapse of any form would never happen?

6. To the preacher: do you take seriously the thought that the sermon you are currently working on may be the last sermon you will preach to your congregation? How does that possibility affect the quality of your work?

7. To the listener: do you take seriously the possibility that the sermon you will hear this Sunday may be the last sermon you will ever hear? How does that possibility affect how you listen, and what you do with the sermon?

Chapter 13

Closing the Letter

As was his custom, Paul closed his letter to Titus with a word of greeting (3:15):

> 15 All who are with me send greetings to you. Greet those who love us in the faith.
> Grace be with you all.

Archaeologists have uncovered hundreds upon hundreds of letters that Greeks wrote to one another in the days of the New Testament. These letters customarily ended with a term that translates as "be strong" or "thrive" or "prosper." The letter from the Jerusalem Council to the churches ended with that customary ending (Acts 15:29). All the standard English Bibles render the term as "Farewell."

Of the thirteen letters we have from the Apostle Paul, however, not one concludes with that customary ending. Instead, Paul typically concludes his letters with three basic components:

- Greetings to the reader(s) from himself and/or those with him,
- The instruction to greet those with his reader(s),
- A word of blessing.

All three are present in his closing words to Titus.

Greetings

The greeting Paul sent to Titus receives color from the actions described at Paul's departure from Ephesus. After he had prayed with the saints, "there was much weeping on the part of all; they embraced Paul and kissed him . . . and accompanied him to the ship" (Acts 20:36–38).

Paul had interacted with Titus through his letter, but as he now took leave of his "true child in a common faith" (Titus 1:4) he could obviously not embrace and kiss him. So what he would otherwise communicate through a physical embrace and a kiss is now communicated through a word: "greetings." It is the expression of care and love and support that we also seek to communicate at a departure.

It is striking to note, then, that in this letter Paul does not extend *personal* greetings to Titus. Those "with" Paul "send greetings to" Titus (3:15). We can only guess who might be "with" Paul. Are these the companions who are currently travelling with Paul on his missionary journey? Are these the brethren of the church where he is laboring while he wrote this letter? Does Titus even know who these people are, let alone know them personally? We have no way of telling.

In fact, if we needed to know the Holy Spirit would have told us. The fact that he did not tell us indicates that something else is more important here than the names of those who extend greetings. What is important is that the bond of faith transcends all boundaries. The Lord at the Tower of Babel dispersed ungodly peoples over the face of all the earth (Gen 11:8), and in so doing pitted nation against nation and people against people in distrust and suspicion. But one chapter later God told Abram that "in you all the families of the earth shall be blessed" (Gen 12:3). Over the years and centuries that followed, the Lord did his work of redemption so that people from any tribe and race were registered on high as born in Zion (Ps 87:6). After the outpouring of the Holy Spirit on Pentecost the Lord worked in the hearts of peoples of any nationality so that they were united by one faith in one Savior.

That thought received concrete expression in Paul's words to Titus: "all who are with me"—irrespective of where they are from—"send greetings to you."

Greet

The same glorious reality informs Paul's last instruction to Titus: "Greet those who love us in the faith." The term "love" here will include one's appreciation for Paul's status as "a servant of God and an apostle of Jesus Christ" (Titus 1:1), and so include one's love for the preaching with which Paul "had been entrusted by the command of God our Savior" (1:3). "Those who love us in the faith" are Cretans who by nature "are always liars, evil beasts, lazy gluttons" (1:12), but now have been changed by the Holy Spirit to "renounce ungodliness and worldly passions" (2:11). They are not at all perfected yet, which is why Titus had so much work to do to complete what was left unfinished in the churches of the island (1:5). Yet Paul recognizes the unity of faith and wants that recognition driven home to the brethren of the island. Paul the Jew greets Gentile Cretans; Paul the zealot for the Law (Phil 3:5–6) greets folk raised to be "liars, evil beasts, lazy gluttons" (1:12). Paul the Apostle is considerably more schooled and advanced in the Lord's service than these new believers on Crete—but he does not hesitate to tell Titus to "greet those who love us in the faith." Each Christian on the island, then, must consider that he has received a personal virtual embrace from the Apostle himself. We well realize that such a greeting provides great encouragement for the "older men," the "older women," the "young women," the "younger men" and the "slaves" of the island who were on the receiving end of Titus' teaching and now see their life's work laid out before them. More, here is great encouragement for the "elders" of each town as they seek to shepherd sinful sheep in a culture of deceit and selfishness. That the "slave of God" would embrace them, the apostle whom Jesus Christ has called to bring them the faith—ah, yes, that is so very, very encouraging! In his embrace is something of the embrace of Jesus Christ himself!

Grace

Paul's final word to Titus is typical of the way the Apostle closes his letters: "Grace be with you all." The word "you" this time, in distinction from its use earlier in the verse, is now written in plural form in Greek, and so extends beyond the direct addressee of the letter, Titus himself. We can imagine, then, that as Titus passes on greetings from Paul to "those who love us in the faith," he may share with them also Paul's prayer and conviction that God's grace is with all of them.

The term "grace" catches the notion of God's free favor to unworthy sinners. Though created "very good" (Gen 1:31), the human race rebelled against God in favor of alignment with the Evil One. God's response was one of "grace": he promised to send his only Son into the world to take on himself the just penalty transgressors deserved—so that in turn these sinners might receive mercy. This is the good news of redemption embedded in the gospel promise first given in Genesis 3:15, and illustrated and proclaimed through the sacrifices and ceremonies of the Law given to Israel at Mt Sinai. This is the same gospel fulfilled through Christ's sacrifice on the cross of Calvary—the same Christ who grabbed Paul by the scruff of his neck on the road to Damascus and compelled him to be his preacher of good tidings to the Gentiles (Acts 9:15; Titus 1:3). The Christians of Crete had embraced this gospel of "grace" so that they now awaited "our blessed hope, the appearing of the glory of our great God and Savior Jesus Christ, who gave himself for us to redeem us from all lawlessness" (2:13–14).

This "grace," of course, is a marvel. No sinner deserves it, and surely not the Cretans either. "Cretans are always liars, evil beasts, lazy gluttons" (1:12), and lying is manifestly of the devil "for he is a liar and the father of lies" (John 8:44)—as Jesus so poignantly put it. More, among the Christians of Crete "there are many who are insubordinate, empty talkers and deceivers" (1:10)—and so, despite the initial work of the Holy Spirit in their hearts, still so undeserving of any "grace." The "training" to "renounce ungodliness and worldly passions" (2:12) is still so very much a work in progress! Yet Paul assures Titus: "Grace be with you all." How marvelous indeed!

Prayer or Reality?

In our English translations, this "grace" is connected to the Cretans ("with you") by means of the verb "be." The word "be" communicates to the reader that Paul is here expressing a wish or a hope that God's "grace" will in fact be with the believers of Crete. Whether the Cretans will in turn experience or receive this grace would then depend on whether they (in keeping with the promises of the covenant) continue to walk in step with the gospel of redemption.

As it is, the Greek does not use a verb here at all. Paul simply says: "Grace with you all." By omitting the verb the Apostle makes clear that God's grace is an enduring reality for these Cretans. God, after all, has begun a work in their midst, and what he has begun he will complete (Ps 138:8). Titus has to "appoint elders in every town" (Titus 1:5) not because Paul fears that Christ's work on the island is about to implode, but because he sees progress in Christ's church work there; that is why what was yet (organizationally) incomplete needs to be put in order. Similarly, Titus has to "teach what accords with sound doctrine" (2:1) not because Paul has no confidence in the future of the church on the island, but because the growth Christ has worked needs further watering (cf. 1 Cor 3:6, 9). Paul is optimistic because he has confidence in his God and Savior! Since God's grace is present reality for the saints of the island, Titus should not be afraid to reassure the believers of that good news: *Grace is with you all!*

Titus

In fact, as Titus packs his bags and rounds off his work on the island, here is delightful encouragement for this faithful laborer. It could not have been easy for Titus to leave, given that there remained so much yet to do in Crete. But departure is surely made easier as Titus hears and knows that "grace" is "with . . . all" the brethren, himself included. He himself may leave the island, but the God of grace does not!

POINTS FOR DISCUSSION

1. Paul typically ends his letters by sending a greeting.

    a. What is the meaning of his greeting?

    b. How does Paul's habit instruct us in what we (should) say and/or do when we part ways with another—be it physically or via letter?

2. Is it acceptable, or even right, to "greet" strangers? Why or why not?

3. Paul tells Titus to pass on greetings to the fellow Christians on the island.

    a. What impact would such a greeting have on Titus' hearers? Think of the elders, the older men, the older women, the younger, etc.

    b. How do you respond when you receive greetings from another, be he known or unknown? How should you respond?

4. How is Paul's typical closing to his letters ("Grace be with you") a better ending than those common in Paul's day ("Farewell")? Draw out the encouragement you receive from the phrase "Grace be with you."

5. Does Paul intend the phrase to be a prayer or a reality? What difference does it make? How do you pick up your minister's closing words?

Index

Index

Index of Scripture References

Index of Scripture References

Leviticus

Numbers

Deuteronomy

Joshua

1 Samuel

2 Samuel

1 Chronicles

Job

Psalms

Proverbs

Index of Scripture References

Index of Scripture References

Index of Scripture References